Dinosaurs: A Very Short Introduction

VERY SHORT INTRODUCTIONS are for anyone wanting a stimulating and accessible way in to a new subject. They are written by experts, and have been published in more than 25 languages worldwide.

The series began in 1995, and now represents a wide variety of topics in history, philosophy, religion, science, and the humanities. Over the next few years it will grow to a library of around 200 volumes – a Very Short Introduction to everything from ancient Egypt and Indian philosophy to conceptual art and cosmology.

Very Short Introductions available now:

For more information visit our web site
www.oup.co.uk/vsi/

David Norman

DINOSAURS

A Very Short Introduction

OXFORD
UNIVERSITY PRESS

OXFORD

UNIVERSITY PRESS

Great Clarendon Street, Oxford OX2 6DP

Oxford University Press is a department of the University of Oxford.
It furthers the University's objective of excellence in research, scholarship,
and education by publishing worldwide in

Oxford New York

Auckland Cape Town Dar es Salaam Hong Kong Karachi
Kuala Lumpur Madrid Melbourne Mexico City Nairobi
New Delhi Shanghai Taipei Toronto

With offices in

Argentina Austria Brazil Chile Czech Republic France Greece
Guatemala Hungary Italy Japan Poland Portugal Singapore
South Korea Switzerland Thailand Turkey Ukraine Vietnam

Oxford is a registered trade mark of Oxford University Press
in the UK and in certain other countries

Published in the United States
by Oxford University Press Inc., New York

British Library Cataloguing in Publication Data

Data available

Library of Congress Cataloging in Publication Data

Data available

ISBN 0-19-280419-7

1 3 5 7 9 10 8 6 4 2

Typeset by RefineCatch Ltd, Bungay, Suffolk
Printed in Great Britain by
TJ International Ltd., Padstow, Cornwall

Contents

List of illustrations

The publisher and the author apologize for any errors or omissions in the above list. If contacted they will be pleased to rectify these at the earliest opportunity.

Introduction

Dinosaurs: facts and fiction

Dinosaurs were 'borne' officially in 1842 as a result of some truly brilliant and intuitive detective work by the British anatomist Richard Owen (Figure 1), whose work had concentrated upon the unique nature of some extinct British fossil reptiles.

At the time of Owen's review, he was working on a surprisingly meagre collection of fossil bones and teeth that had been discovered up to that time and were scattered around the British Isles. Although the birth of dinosaurs was relatively inauspicious (first appearing as an afterthought in the published report of the 11th meeting of the British Association for the Advancement of Science), they were soon to become the centre of worldwide attention. The reason for this was simple. Owen worked in London, at the Museum of the Royal College of Surgeons, at a time when the British Empire was probably at its greatest extent. To celebrate such influence and achievement, the Great Exhibition of 1851 was devised. To house this event a huge temporary exhibition hall (Joseph Paxton's steel and glass 'Crystal Palace') was built on Hyde Park in central London.

Rather than destroy the wonderful exhibition hall at the end of 1851 it was moved to a permanent site at the London suburb of

1. Professor Richard Owen (1804–92)

Sydenham (the future Crystal Palace Park). The parkland surrounding the exhibition building was landscaped and arranged thematically, and one of the themes depicted scientific endeavour in the form of natural history and geology and how they had contributed to unravelling the Earth's history. This geological theme park, probably one of the earliest of its kind, included reconstructions of genuine geological features (caves, limestone pavements, geological strata) as well as representations of the inhabitants of the ancient world. Owen, in collaboration with the sculptor and entrepreneur Benjamin Waterhouse Hawkins, populated the parkland with gigantic iron-framed and concrete-clad models of dinosaurs (Figure 2) and other prehistoric creatures known at this time. The advance publicity generated before the relocated 'Great Exhibition' was re-opened in June 1854 included a celebratory dinner held on New Year's Eve 1853 within the belly of a half-completed model of the dinosaur *Iguanodon* and this ensured considerable public awareness of Owen's dinosaurs.

The fact that dinosaurs were extinct denizens of hitherto unsuspected earlier worlds, and were the literal embodiment of the dragons of myth and legend, probably guaranteed their adoption by society at large; they even appeared in the works of Charles Dickens, who was a personal acquaintance of Richard Owen. From such evocative beginnings public interest in dinosaurs has been nurtured and maintained ever since. Quite why the appeal should have been so persistent has been much speculated upon; it may have much to do with the importance of story-telling as a means of stimulating human imaginative and creative abilities. It strikes me as no coincidence that in humans the most formative years of intellectual growth and cultural development, between the ages of about 3 and 10 years, are often those when the enthusiasm for dinosaurs is greatest – as many parents can testify. The buzz of excitement created when children glimpse their first dinosaur skeleton is almost palpable. Dinosaurs, as the late Stephen Jay Gould – arguably our greatest popularizer of scientific natural history – memorably remarked, are popular because they are 'big, scary and [fortunately for us] dead', and it is true that their gaunt skeletons exert a gravitational pull on the imaginative landscape of youngsters.

A remarkable piece of evidence in support of the notion that there is a relationship between the latent appeal of dinosaurs and the human psyche can be found in mythology and folklore. Adrienne

2. Top: a sketch of the *Iguanodon* model at Crystal Palace.
Bottom: A photograph of the model of *Megalosaurus* in Crystal Palace
Park.

Mayor has shown that as early as the 7th century BC the Greeks had contact with nomadic cultures in central Asia. Written accounts at this time include descriptions of the Griffin (or Gryphon): a creature that reputedly hoarded and jealously guarded gold; it was wolf-sized with a beak, four legs, and sharp claws on its feet. Furthermore, Near East art of at least 3000 BC depicts Griffin-like creatures, as does that of the Mycenaean. The Griffin myth arose in Mongolia/north-west China, in association with the ancient caravan routes and gold prospecting in the Tienshan and Altai Mountains. This part of the world (we now know) has a very rich fossil heritage and is notable for the abundance of well-preserved dinosaur skeletons; they are remarkably easy to find because their white fossil bones stand out clearly against the soft, red sandstones in which they are buried. Of even greater interest is the fact that the most abundant of the dinosaurs preserved in these sandstones is *Protoceratops*, which are approximately wolf-sized, and have a prominent hooked beak and four legs terminated by sharp-clawed toes. Their skulls also bear strikingly upswept bony frills, which might easily be the origin of the wing-like structures that are often depicted in Griffin imagery (compare the images in Figure 3). Griffins were reported and figured very consistently for more than a millennium, but beyond the 3rd century AD they became defined increasingly by allegorical traits. On this basis it would appear to be highly probable that Griffins owe their origin to genuine observations of dinosaur skeletons made by nomadic travellers through Mongolia; they demonstrate an uncanny link between exotic mythological beasts and the real world of dinosaurs.

Looked at through the harsh lens of objectivity, the cultural pervasiveness of dinosaurs is extraordinary. After all, no human being has ever seen a living non-avian dinosaur (no matter what some of the more absurd creationist literature might claim). The very first recognizably human members of our species lived about 500,000 years ago. By contrast, the very last dinosaurs trod our planet approximately 65 million years ago and probably perished,

3. The Griffin of mythology exhibits all the key anatomical attributes of *Protoceratops*, whose skeletons would have been observed by travellers on the Silk Road through Mongolia

along with many other creatures, in a cataclysm following a giant meteorite impact with Earth at that time (see Chapter 8). Dinosaurs, as a group of animals of quite bewildering variety, therefore existed on Earth for over 160 million years *before* their sudden demise. This surely puts the span of human existence, and our current dominance of this fragile planet (in particular, the debates concerning our utilization of resources, pollution, and global warming), into a decidedly sobering perspective.

The very fact of the recognition of dinosaurs, and the very different world in which they lived, today is a testament to the extraordinary explanatory power of science. The ability to be inquisitive, to probe the natural world and all its products, and to keep asking that beguilingly simple question – why? – is one of the essences of being human. It is hardly surprising that developing rigorous methods in order to determine answers to such general questions is at the core of all science.

Dinosaurs are undeniably interesting to many people. Their very existence incites curiosity, and this can be used in some instances as a means of introducing unsuspecting audiences to the excitement of scientific discovery and the application and use of science more generally. Just as fascination with bird songs could lead to an interest in the physics of sound transmission, echolocation, and ultimately radar, on the one hand, or linguistics and psychology on the other; so it can be that an interest in dinosaurs can open pathways into an equally surprising and unexpectedly wide range of scientific disciplines. Outlining some of these pathways into science is one of the underlying purposes of this book.

Palaeontology is the science that has been built around the study of fossils, the remains of organisms that died prior to the time when human culture began to have an identifiable impact on the world, that is more than 10,000 years ago. This branch of science represents our attempt to bring such fossils back to life: not literally, as in resuscitating dead creatures (in the fictional *Jurassic Park* mode), but by using science to understand as fully as we can what such creatures were really like and how they fitted into their world. When a fossil of an animal is discovered, it presents the palaeontologist with a series of puzzles, not unlike those faced by the fictional sleuth Sherlock Holmes:

- What type of creature was it when it was alive?
- How long ago did it die?
- Did it die naturally of old age, or was it killed?
- Did it die just where it was found, buried in the rock, or was its body moved here from somewhere else?
- Was it male or female?
- How did the creature look when it was alive?
- Was it colourful or drab?
- Was it fast-moving or a slow-coach?
- What did it eat?
- How well could it see, smell, or hear?
- Is it related to any creatures that are alive today?

These are just a few examples of the questions that might be asked, but all tend towards the piecemeal reconstruction of a picture of the creature and of the world in which it lived. It has been my experience, following on from the first broadcasting of the television series called *Walking with Dinosaurs*, with their incredibly realistic-looking virtual dinosaurs, that many people were sufficiently intrigued by what they saw or heard in the commentary to ask: 'How did you know that they moved like that? . . . looked like that? . . . behaved like that?'

Questions driven by uncomplicated observations and basic common sense underpin this book. Every fossil discovery is in and of itself unique and has the potential to teach the inquisitive among us something about our heritage as members of our world. I should, however, qualify this statement by adding that the particular type of heritage that I will be discussing relates to the *natural* heritage that we share with all other organisms on this planet. This natural heritage spans a period of time that exceeds 3,800 million years according to most modern estimates. I will be exploring only a tiny section of this staggeringly long period of time: just that interval between 225 and 65 million years ago, when dinosaurs dominated most aspects of life on Earth.

Chapter 1
Dinosaurs in perspective

The fossilized remains of dinosaurs (with the notable exception of their lineal descendants the birds – see Chapter 6) have been found in rocks identified as belonging to the Mesozoic Era. Mesozoic rocks range in age from 245 to 65 million years ago (abbreviated to Ma from now on). In order to put the time during which dinosaurs lived into context, since such numbers are so large as to be quite literally unimaginable, it is simpler to refer the reader to the geological timescale (Figure 4).

During the 19th and a considerable part of the 20th centuries, the age of the Earth, and the relative ages of the different rocks of which it is composed, had been the subject of intense scrutiny. During the early part of the 19th century it was becoming recognized (though not without dispute) that the rocks of the Earth, and the fossils that they contained, could be divided into qualitatively different types. There were rocks that appeared to contain no fossils (often referred to as igneous, or 'basement'). Positioned above these apparently lifeless basement rocks was a sequence of four types of rocks that signified four ages of the Earth. During much of the 19th century these were named Primary, Secondary, Tertiary, and Quaternary – quite literally the first, second, third, and fourth ages. The ones that contained traces of ancient shelled and simple fish-like creatures were 'Primary' (now more commonly called Palaeozoic, literally indicative of 'ancient life'). Above the palaeozoics was a sequence of rocks that contained a combination of shells, fish, and land-living saurians (or 'crawlers', which today would include amphibians and reptiles); these rocks were designated broadly as 'Secondary' (nowadays Mesozoic, 'middle life'). Above the mesozoics were found rocks that contain creatures more similar to those living today, notably because they include mammals and birds; these were named 'Tertiary' (now also called Cenozoic, 'recent life'). And finally, there was the 'Quaternary' (or Recent) that charted the appearance of recognizably modern plants and animals and the influence of the great ice ages.

This general pattern has stood the test of time remarkably well. All modern geological timescales continue to recognize these relatively crude, but fundamental, subdivisions: Paleozoic, Mesozoic, Cenozoic, Recent. However, refinements in the way the fossil record can be examined for example, through the use of high-resolution microscopy, the identification of chemical signatures associated with life, and the more accurate dating of rocks enabled by radioactive isotope techniques have led to a more precise timescale of Earth history.

The part of the timescale that we are most concerned with in this book is the Mesozoic Era, comprising three geological periods: the Triassic (245–200 Ma), the Jurassic (200–144 Ma), and the Cretaceous (144–65 Ma). Note that these periods of time are not by any means equal in duration. Geologists were not able to identify a metronome-like tick of the clock measuring the passing of Earth time. The boundaries between the periods were mapped out in the last two centuries by geologists who were able to define particular rock types and, very often, their constituent fossils, and this is usually reflected in the names chosen for the periods. The term 'Triassic' originates from a triplet of distinctive rock types (known as the Lias, Malm, and Dogger); the 'Jurassic' hails from a sequence of rocks identified in the Jura Mountains of France; while the name 'Cretaceous' was chosen to reflect the great thickness of chalk (known as Kreta in Greek) such as that which

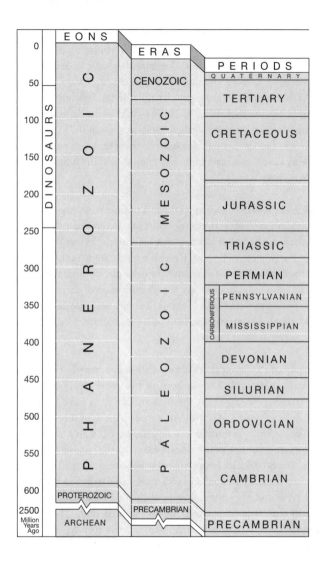

4. The geological timescale puts into context the period during which the dinosaurs lived on Earth

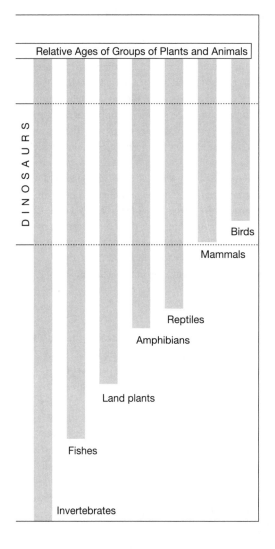

Relative Ages of Groups of Plants and Animals

DINOSAURS

Birds

Mammals

Reptiles

Amphibians

Land plants

Fishes

Invertebrates

forms the White Cliffs of Dover and is found widely across Eurasia and North America.

The earliest dinosaurs known have been identified in rocks dated at 225 Ma, from the close of the Triassic (a period known as the Carnian), in Argentina and Madagascar. Rather disconcertingly, these earliest remains are not rare, solitary examples of one type of creature: the common ancestor of all later dinosaurs. To date at least four, possibly five, different creatures have been identified: three meat-eaters (*Eoraptor*, *Herrerasaurus*, and *Staurikosaurus*), a tantalizingly incomplete plant-eater named *Pisanosaurus*, and an as-yet-unnamed omnivore. One conclusion is obvious: these are *not* the earliest dinosaurs. In the Carnian there was clearly a diversity of early dinosaurs. This indicates that there must have been dinosaurs living in the Middle Triassic (Ladinian-Anisian) that had 'fathered' the Carnian diversity. So we know for a fact that the story of dinosaur origins, both the time and the place, is incomplete.

Why dinosaur fossils are rare

It is important, at the outset, for the reader to realize that the fossil record is incomplete and, perhaps more worryingly, decidedly patchy. The incompleteness is a product of the process of fossilization. Dinosaurs were all land-living (terrestrial) animals, which poses particular problems. To appreciate this, it is necessary first to consider the case of a shelled creature living in the sea, such as an oyster. In the shallow seas where oysters live today, their fossilization potential is quite high. They are living on, or attached to, the seabed and are subjected to a constant 'drizzle' of small particles (sediment), including decaying planktonic organisms, silt or mud, and sand grains. If an oyster should die, its soft tissues would rot or be scavenged by other organisms quite quickly and its hard shell would be gradually buried under fine sediment. Once buried, the shell has the potential to become a fossil as it becomes trapped under an increasingly thick layer of sediment. Over thousands or millions of years, the sediment in which the shell was

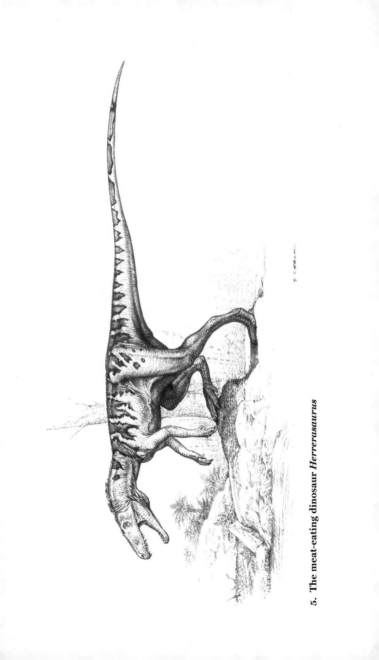

5. The meat-eating dinosaur *Herrerasaurus*

buried is gradually compressed to form a silty sandstone, and this may become cemented or lithified (literally, turned to stone) by the deposition of calcium carbonate (calcite) or silica (chert/flint) carried through the fabric of the rock by percolating water. For the fossil remains of the original oyster to be discovered, the deeply buried rock would need to be lifted, by earth movements, to form dry land, and then subjected to the normal processes of weathering and erosion.

Land-living creatures, by contrast, have a far lower probability of becoming fossilized. Any animal dying on land is likely, of course, to have its soft, fleshy remains scavenged and recycled; however, for such a creature to be preserved as a fossil it would need to be subject to some form of burial. In rare circumstances creatures may be buried rapidly in drifting dune sand, a mud-slide, under volcanic ash, or some by other catastrophic event. However, in the majority of cases the remains of land animals need to be washed into a nearby stream or river, and eventually find their way into a lake or seabed where the process of slow burial, leading to fossilization, can commence. In simple, probabilistic terms the pathway to fossilization for any land creature is that much longer, and fraught with greater hazard. Many animals that die on land are scavenged and their remains become entirely scattered so that even their hard parts are recycled into the biosphere; others have their skeletons scattered, so that only broken fragments actually complete the path to eventual burial, leaving tantalizing glimpses of creatures; only very rarely will major parts, or even whole skeletons, be preserved in their entirety.

So, logic dictates that dinosaur skeletons (as with any land-living animal) should be extremely rare and so they are, despite the impression sometimes given by the media.

The discovery of dinosaurs and their appearance within the fossil record is also a decidedly patchy business, for rather mundane reasons. Fossil preservation is, as we have just come to appreciate, a chance-laden, rather than design-driven, process. The discovery of fossils is similarly serendipitous in the sense that outcrops of rocks are not neatly arranged like the pages of a book to be sampled perhaps in sequence, or as fancy takes us.

The relatively brittle surface layers of the Earth (its crust, in geological terms) have been buckled, torn, and crumpled by huge geological forces acting over tens or hundreds of millions of years that have wrenched landmasses apart or crushed them together. As a result, the geological strata containing fossils have been broken, thrown up, and frequently destroyed completely by the process of erosion throughout geological time, and further confused by later periods of renewed sedimentation. What we, as palaeontologists, are left with is an extremely complex 'battlefield', pitted, cratered, and broken in a bewildering variety of ways. Disentangling this 'mess' has been the work of countless generations of field geologists. Outcrops here, cliff-sections there, have been studied and slowly assembled into the jigsaw that is the geological structure of the land. As a result, it is now possible to identify rocks of Mesozoic age (belonging to the Triassic, Jurassic, and Cretaceous Periods) with some accuracy in any country in the world. However, that is not sufficient to aid the search for dinosaurs. It is also necessary to disregard Mesozoic rocks laid down on the sea floor, such as the thick chalk deposits of the Cretaceous and the abundant limestones of the Jurassic. The best types of rocks to search in for dinosaur fossils are those that were laid down as shallow coastal or estuarine environments; these might have trapped the odd, bloated carcasses of land-living creatures washed out to sea. But best of all are river and lake sediments, environments that were physically much closer to the source of land creatures.

Searching for dinosaurs

From the very outset, we need to approach the search for dinosaurs systematically. On the basis of what we have learned so far, it is first necessary to check where to find rocks of the appropriate age by consulting geological maps of the country that is of interest. It is equally important to ensure that the rocks are of a type that is at least likely to preserve the remains of land animals; so some geological knowledge is required in order to predict the likelihood of finding dinosaur fossils, especially when visiting an area for the first time.

Mostly, this involves developing a familiarity with rocks and their appearance in the area being investigated; this is rather similar to the way in which a hunter needs to study intently the terrain in which the prey lives. It also requires the development of an 'eye' for fossils, which comes simply from looking until fossil fragments are eventually recognized, and this takes time.

Discovery provides the adrenaline-rush of excitement, but is also the time when the discoverer needs to be most circumspect. All too often fossil discoveries have been ruined, scientifically speaking, in the frantic rush to dig the specimen up, so that it can be displayed by its proud finder. Such impatience can result in great damage to the fossil itself. Even worse, the object might be part of a larger skeleton that might be far more profitably excavated carefully by a larger team of trained palaeontologists. And, as the sleuth might point out, the rocks in which the fossil was embedded may also have important tales to tell concerning the circumstances under which the animal died and was buried, in addition to the more obvious information concerning the actual geological age of the specimen.

The search for, and discovery of, fossils can be a personally exciting adventure as well as a technically fascinating process. However, finding fossils is just the beginning of a process of scientific investigation that can lead to an understanding of the biology and way of life of the fossilized creature and the world in which it once lived. In this latter respect, the science of palaeontology exhibits some similarities to the work of the forensic pathologist: both clearly share an intense interest in understanding the circumstances surrounding the discovery of a body, and use science to interpret and understand as many of the clues as possible in an effort to leave, quite literally, no stone unturned.

Dinosaur discovery: *Iguanodon*

Once you have found your fossil, it needs to be studied scientifically in order to reveal its identity, its relationship to other known organisms, as well as more detailed aspects of its appearance, biology, and ecology. To illustrate a few of the trials and tribulations inherent in any such programme of palaeontological investigation, we will examine a rather familiar and well-studied dinosaur: *Iguanodon*. This dinosaur has been chosen because it has an interesting and appropriate story to tell, and one with which I am familiar, because it proved to be the unexpected starting point for my career as a palaeontologist. Serendipity seems to have a significant role to play in palaeontology, and this is certainly true for my own work.

The story of *Iguanodon* covers almost the entire history of scientific research on dinosaurs and also the entire history of the science now known as palaeontology. As a result, this animal unwittingly illustrates the progress of scientific investigation on dinosaurs (and other areas of palaeontology) during the past 200 years. The story also reveals scientists as human beings, with passions and struggles, and the pervasive influence of pet theories at times in the history of the subject.

The first *bona fide* records of the fossil bones that were later to be named *Iguanodon* date back to 1809. They comprise, among indeterminable broken fragments of vertebrae, the lower end of a large, very distinctive tibia (shin bone) collected from a quarry at Cuckfield in Sussex (Figure 6). This particular fossil was collected by William Smith (often referred to as the 'father of English geology'). Smith was then researching the first geological map of Britain, which he completed in 1815. Although these fossil bones were clearly sufficiently interesting to have been collected and

6. The first *Iguanodon* bone ever collected, by William Smith at
Cuckfield in Sussex, in 1809

preserved (they are still in the collections of the Natural History Museum, London), no further study was made of them. The bones languished unrecognized until I was asked to establish their identity in the late 1970s.

Yet 1809 was a remarkably opportune moment for such a discovery to be made. Things were happening in Europe in the branch of science concerned with fossils and their meaning. One of the greatest and most influential scientists of this age, Georges Cuvier (1769–1832), was a 'naturalist' working in Paris and an administrator in the Emperor Napoleon's government. 'Naturalist' was, in these times, a broad category denoting the philosopher-scientist who worked on a wide range of subjects associated with the natural world: the Earth, its rocks and minerals, fossils, and all living organisms. In 1808, Cuvier redescribed a renowned gigantic fossil reptile collected from a chalk quarry at Maastricht in Holland; its renown stemmed from the fact that it had been claimed as a trophy of war during the siege of Maastricht in 1795 by Napoleon's army. The creature, originally mistaken for a crocodile, was identified correctly by Cuvier as an enormous marine lizard (later named *Mosasaurus* by the English cleric and naturalist the Revd William D. Conybeare). The effect of this revelation – the existence of an unexpectedly gigantic fossil lizard of a former time in Earth history – was truly profound. It encouraged the search for, and discovery of, other giant extinct 'lizards'; it established, beyond reasonable doubt, that pre-biblical 'earlier worlds' had existed; and it also determined a particular way of viewing and interpreting such fossil creatures: as gigantic lizards.

Following the defeat of Napoleon and the restoration of peace between England and France, Cuvier was finally able to visit England in 1817–18 and meet scientists with similar interests. At Oxford he was shown some gigantic fossil bones in the collections of the geologist William Buckland; these seemed to belong to a gigantic, but this time land-living, lizard-like creature, and they reminded Cuvier of similar bones that had been found in

Normandy. William Buckland eventually named this creature *Megalosaurus* in 1824 (with a little help from Conybeare).

However, from the perspective of this particular story, the really important discoveries were not made until around 1821–2 and at the same quarries, around Whiteman's Green in Cuckfield, visited by William Smith some 13 years earlier. At this time, an energetic and ambitious medical doctor, Gideon Algernon Mantell (1790–1852), living in the town of Lewes, was dedicating all his spare time to completing a detailed report on the geological structure and fossils in his native Weald district (an area incorporating much of Surrey, Sussex, and part of Kent) in southern England. His work culminated in an impressively large, well-illustrated book that he published in 1822. Included in this book were clear descriptions of several unusual, large reptilian teeth and ribs that he had been unable to identify properly. Several of these teeth were purchased by Mantell from quarrymen, while others had been collected by his wife, Mary Ann. The next three years saw Mantell struggling to identify the type of animal to which these large fossil teeth might have belonged. Although not trained in comparative anatomy (the particular specialism of Cuvier), he developed contacts with many learned men in England in the hope of gaining some insight into the affinity of his fossils; he also sent some of his precious specimens to Cuvier in Paris for identification. At first, Mantell's discoveries were dismissed, even by Cuvier, as fragments of Recent animals (perhaps the incisor teeth of a rhinoceros, or those of large, coral-chewing, bony fish). Undeterred, Mantell continued to investigate his problem, and finally found a likely solution. In the collections of the Royal College of Surgeons in London he was shown the skeleton of an iguana, a herbivorous lizard that had recently been discovered in South America. The teeth were similar in general shape to those of his fossils and indicated to Mantell that they belonged to an extinct, herbivorous, giant relative of the living iguana. Mantell published a report on the new discovery in 1825 and the name chosen for this fossil creature was, perhaps not surprisingly, *Iguanodon*. The name means, quite

7. One of the original *Iguanodon* teeth found by the Mantells

literally, 'iguana tooth' and was created yet again, at the suggestion of Conybeare (clearly the latter's classical training and turn of mind gave him a natural facility in the naming of many of these early discoveries).

Not surprisingly, given the comparisons then available, these early discoveries confirmed the existence of an ancient world inhabited by improbably large lizards. For example, a simple scaling of the minute teeth of the living (metre-long) iguana with those of Mantell's *Iguanodon* yielded a body length in excess of 25 metres. The excitement, and personal fame, engendered by the description of *Iguanodon* drove Mantell to greater efforts to discover more about this animal and the fossil inhabitants of the ancient Weald.

For several years after 1825, only fragments of Weald fossils were discovered; then, in 1834, a partial, disarticulated skeleton (Figure 8) was discovered at a quarry in Maidstone, Kent. Eventually purchased for Mantell, and christened the 'Mantel-piece', it proved to be the inspiration behind much of his later work and resulted in some of the first visualizations of dinosaurs ever produced (Figure 9). He continued probing the anatomy and biology of *Iguanodon* in his later years, but much of this was, alas, overshadowed by the rise of an extremely able, well-connected, ambitious, and ruthless personal nemesis: Richard Owen (1804–1892) (see Figure 1).

The 'invention' of dinosaurs

Fourteen years younger than Mantell, Richard Owen also studied medicine, but concentrated in particular on anatomy. He gained a reputation as a skilled anatomist, and acquired a position at the Royal College of Surgeons in London, which gave him access to a great deal of comparative material and, through considerable industry and skill, allowed him to foster a reputation as the 'English Cuvier'. During the late 1830s, he was able to persuade the British Association to grant him money to prepare a detailed review of all

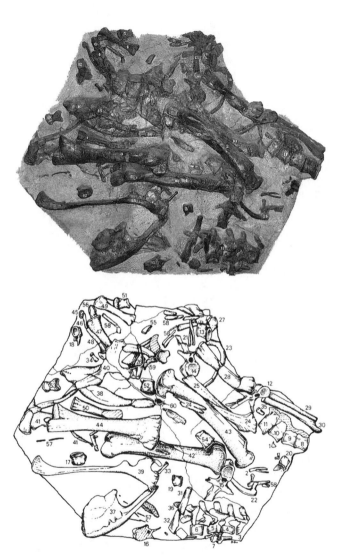

8. Photograph and sketch of 'Mantel-piece', a partial skeleton discovered in Maidstone, Kent, in 1834

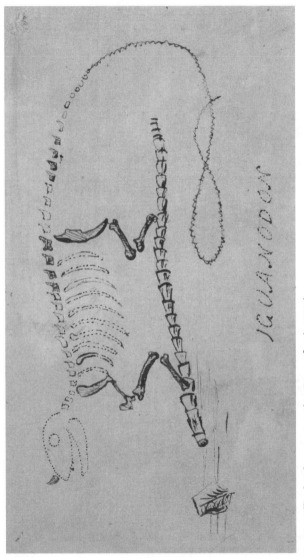

9. Mantell's sketch reconstructing *Iguanodon* (c. 1834)

that was then known of British fossil reptiles. This eventually resulted in the publication of a stream of large, well-illustrated volumes that would mimic the hugely important works (notably the multi–volume *Ossemens Fossiles*) published by Cuvier earlier in the century, and further cemented Owen's scientific reputation.

This project resulted in two important publications: one in 1840 on mostly marine fossils (Conybeare's *Enaliosauria*) and another in 1842 on the remainder, including Mantell's *Iguanodon*. The 1842 report is a remarkable document because of Owen's invention of the new 'tribe or sub-order . . . which I . . . name . . . Dinosauria'. Owen identified three dinosaurs in this report: *Iguanodon* and *Hylaeosaurus*, both discovered in the Weald and named by Mantell; and *Megalosaurus*, the giant reptile from Oxford. He recognized dinosaurs as members of a unique and hitherto unrecognized group on the basis of several detailed and distinctive anatomical observations. These included the enlarged sacrum (a remarkably strong attachment of the hips to the spinal column), the double-headed ribs in the chest region, and the pillar-like construction of the legs (see Figure 10).

In reviewing each dinosaur in turn, Owen trimmed their dimensions considerably, suggesting that they were large, but in the

10. Owen's reconstruction of *Megalosaurus* (c. 1854)

region of 9 to 12 metres, rather than the more dramatic lengths suggested by Cuvier, Mantell, and Buckland on previous occasions. Furthermore, Owen speculated a little more on the anatomy and biology of these animals in words that have an extraordinary resonance in the light of today's interpretations of the biology and way of life of dinosaurs.

Among his concluding remarks in the report, he observed that dinosaurs:

> attained the greatest bulk, and must have played the most conspicuous parts, in their respective characters as devourers of animals and feeders upon vegetables, that this earth has ever witnessed in oviparous [egg-laying] and cold-blooded creatures.
>
> (Owen 1842: 200)

And also that:

> The Dinosaurs having the same thoracic structure as the Crocodile, may be concluded to have possessed a four-chambered heart ... more nearly approaching that which now characterizes the warm-blooded Mammalia.
>
> (ibid.: 204)

Owen's conception was therefore one of very stout, but egg-laying and scaly (because they were still reptiles) creatures resembling the largest mammals to be found in the tropical regions of the Earth today; his dinosaurs were in effect the crowning glory of a time on Earth when egg-laying and scaly-skinned reptiles reigned supreme. Owen's dinosaurs were the ancient world's equivalents of present-day elephants, rhinos, and hippos. Looked at purely from the logic of scientific deduction, based on such meagre remains, this was not only brilliantly incisive, but an altogether revolutionary vision of creatures from the ancient past. Such breathtaking vision is all the more remarkable when it is juxtaposed to the 'gigantic lizard' models, though these were entirely reasonable and logical interpretations built on established and respected Cuvierian principles of comparative anatomy.

The creation of the Dinosauria had other important purposes at the time. The reports also offered a sweeping refutation of the general progressionist and transmutationist movements within the fields of biology and geology during the first half of the 19th century. Progressionists noted that the fossil record seemed to show that life had become progressively more complex: the earliest rocks showed the simplest forms of life, while more recent rocks showed evidence of more complex creatures. Transmutationists noted that members of one species were not identical and pondered whether this variability might also allow species to change over time. Jean Baptiste de Lamarck, a colleague of Cuvier in Paris, had suggested that animal species might transmute, or change, in form over time through the inheritance of acquired characteristics. These ideas challenged the widely held, biblically inspired belief that God had created all creatures on Earth, and were being widely and acrimoniously discussed.

Dinosaurs, and indeed several of the groups of organisms recognized in the God-fearing Owen's reports, provided evidence that life on Earth did not demonstrate an increase in complexity over time – in fact quite the reverse. Dinosaurs were anatomically reptiles (that is to say, members of the general group of egg-laying, cold-blooded, scaly vertebrates); however, the reptiles living today were a degenerate group of creatures when compared to Owen's magnificent dinosaurs that had lived during Mesozoic times. In short, Owen was attempting to strangle the radical, scientifically driven intellectualism of the time in order to re-establish an understanding of the diversity of life that had its basis closer to the views espoused by Reverend William Paley in his book entitled *Natural Theology* in which God held centre-stage as the Creator and Architect of all Nature's creatures.

Owen's fame grew steadily through the 1840s and 1850s, and he became involved in the committees associated with the planning of the relocated Great Exhibition of 1854. It is a curious fact that Owen, for all his burgeoning fame, was not first choice as the scientific director for the construction of the dinosaurs – Gideon Mantell was. Mantell refused on the grounds of persistent ill-health, and also because he was exceedingly wary of the risks associated with popularizing scientific work, particularly the risk of misrepresentating imperfectly developed ideas.

Mantell's story ended in tragedy: his obsession with fossils and the development of a personal museum led to the collapse of his medical practice, and his family disintegrated (his wife left him and his surviving children emigrated once they were old enough to leave home). The diary that he kept for much of his life makes melancholy reading; in his final years he was left lonely and racked by chronic back pain, and he died of a self-administered overdose of laudanum.

Although outflanked by the ambitious, brilliant, and crucially full-time, scientist Owen, Mantell spent much of the last decade of his life continuing research on 'his' *Iguanodon*. He produced a series of scientific articles and extremely popular books summarizing many of his new discoveries, and he was the first to realize (in 1851) that Owen's vision of the dinosaurs (or at least *Iguanodon*) as stout 'elephantine reptiles' was probably wrong. Further discoveries of jaws with teeth, and further analysis of the partial skeleton (the 'Mantel-piece'), revealed that *Iguanodon* had strong back legs and smaller, weaker front limbs. As a result, he concluded that its posture may have had much more in common with the 'upright' reconstructions of giant ground sloths (paradoxically inspired by Owen's detailed description of the fossil ground sloth *Mylodon*). Unfortunately, this work was overlooked, largely because of the excitement and publicity surrounding Owen's Crystal Palace dinosaur models. The truth of Mantell's suspicions, and the strength of his own intellect, were not to be revealed for a further 30 years, and through another amazing piece of serendipity.

Reconstructing *Iguanodon*

In 1878 remarkable discoveries were made at a coal mine in the small village of Bernissart in Belgium. The colliers, who were mining a coal seam over 300 metres beneath the surface, suddenly struck a seam of shale (soft, laminated clay) and began to find what appeared to be large pieces of fossil wood; these were eagerly collected because they seemed to be filled with gold! On closer inspection, the wood turned out to be fossil bone, and the gold 'fool's gold' (iron pyrites). A few fossil teeth were also discovered among the bones, and these were identified as similar to those described as belonging to *Iguanodon* by Mantell many years before. The miners had accidentally discovered not gold, but a veritable treasure trove of complete dinosaur skeletons.

Over the next five years, a team of miners and scientists from the Royal Belgian Museum of Natural History in Brussels (now the

11. Louis Dollo (1857–1931)

Royal Institute of Natural Sciences) excavated nearly 40 skeletons of the dinosaur *Iguanodon*, as well as a huge number of other animals and plants whose remains were preserved in the same shales. Many of the dinosaur skeletons were complete and fully articulated; they represented the most spectacular discovery that had been made anywhere in the world at the time. It was the good fortune of a young scientist in Brussels, Louis Dollo (1857–1931), to be able to study and describe these extraordinary riches, and this he did from 1882 until his retirement in the 1920s.

The complete dinosaur skeletons unearthed in Bernissart proved finally that Owen's model of dinosaurs such as *Iguanodon* was incorrect. As Mantell had suspected, the front limbs were not as large and strong as the back legs, while the animal had a massive tail (see Figure 12), and the overall proportions of a giant kangaroo.

The skeletal restoration, and the process by which it was arrived at, are particularly revealing because they show how the influence of

12. Drawing of an *Iguanodon* skeleton

the contemporary interpretations about the appearance and affinities of dinosaurs affected Dollo's work. Owen's 'elephantine reptile' vision of the dinosaur had been questioned as early as 1859 by some tantalizingly incomplete dinosaur discoveries made in New Jersey and studied by Joseph Leidy, a man of equivalent scientific stature to Owen who was based at the Philadelphia Academy of Natural Sciences. However, Owen was to be far more roundly criticized by a younger, London-based, and ambitious rival: Thomas Henry Huxley (1825–95).

By the late 1860s, a series of new discoveries had been made that added considerably to the debate over the relationships of dinosaurs to other animals. The earliest well-preserved fossil bird (called *Archaeopteryx*, or 'ancient wing') had been discovered in Germany (Figure 13). It was eventually bought from its private collector by the Natural History Museum in London, and described by Richard Owen in 1863. The specimen was unusual in that it had well-preserved impressions of feathers, the key identifier for any bird, forming a halo in the matrix around its skeleton; however, unlike any living bird, and rather disconcertingly similar to modern reptiles, it also had three long fingers ending in sharp claws on each hand, teeth in its jaws, and a long bony tail (some living birds might seem to have long tails, but this is just the profile of their feathers that are anchored in a short remnant of the tail).

Not long after the discovery of *Archaeopteryx*, another small, well-preserved skeleton was found in the same quarries in Germany (Figure 14). It bore no feather impressions and its arms were far too short to have served as wings in any case; anatomically, it was clearly a small, predatory dinosaur and was named *Compsognathus* ('pretty jaw').

These two discoveries emerged at a particularly sensitive time scientifically speaking. In 1859, just a year or so before the first skeleton of *Archaeopteryx* was unearthed, Charles Darwin published a book entitled *On the Origin of Species*. This book

13. A well preserved *Archaeopteryx* specimen, discovered in 1876 (approx 40 cm long)

provided a very detailed discussion of the evidence in favour of the ideas being put forward by the transmutationists and progressionists referred to earlier. Most importantly, Darwin suggested a mechanism – natural selection – by which such transmutations might occur and how new species appear on Earth. The book was sensational at the time because it offered a direct challenge to the almost universally accepted authority of biblical teachings by suggesting that God did not directly create all the

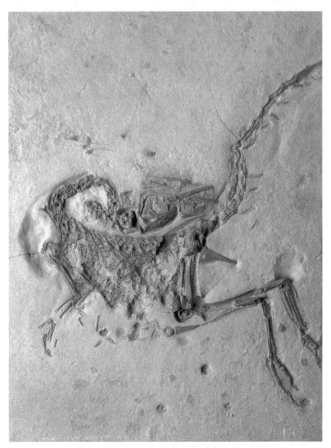

14. *Compsognathus* skeleton (approx 70 cm long)

species known in the world. Darwin's ideas were vigorously opposed by pious establishment figures such as Richard Owen. In contrast, the radical intellectuals reacted very positively to Darwin's ideas. Thomas Huxley is reputed to have declared, after reading Darwin's book, 'How very stupid of me not to have thought of that!'

While not wishing to become too involved in Darwinian matters, it is nevertheless the case that dinosaurian discoveries featured in some of the arguments. Huxley was quick to realize that *Archaeopteryx* and the small predatory dinosaur *Compsognathus* were anatomically very similar. By the early 1870s, Huxley was proposing that birds and dinosaurs were not only anatomically similar, but used this evidence to support the theory that birds had evolved from dinosaurs. In many ways, the stage was set for the discoveries in Belgium. By the late 1870s, Louis Dollo, as a bright young student, would have been fully aware of the Owen–Huxley/ Darwin feuds. One burning question must have been: did these new discoveries have any bearing on the great scientific controversy of the day?

Careful anatomical study of the full skeleton of *Iguanodon* revealed that it had a hip structure known as ornithischian ('bird-hipped'); furthermore, it had long back legs that ended in massive, but decidedly bird-like, three-toed feet (very similar in shape to the feet of some of the biggest known land-living birds such as emus). This dinosaur also had a rather bird-like curved neck, and the tips of its upper and lower jaws were toothless and covered by, yet again, a bird-like horny beak or bill. Given the task of description and interpretation faced by Dollo in the immediate aftermath of these exciting discoveries, it is intriguing to note that, in the early photographs taken at the time of the reconstruction of the first skeleton in Brussels, just beside the huge dinosaur skeleton can be seen skeletons of two Australian creatures: a wallaby (a small variety of kangaroo) and a large, flightless bird known as a cassowary.

The influence of the debate raging in England cannot be doubted. This new discovery pointed to the truth implicit in Huxley's arguments and made it clear that Mantell had been on the right track in 1851. *Iguanodon* was no lumbering, scaly rhinoceros lookalike as portrayed by Owen in his grand models of 1854; rather it was a huge creature with a pose similar to that of a resting

15. *Iguanodon* being reconstructed at the Museum of Natural History, Brussels, in 1878. Note the cassowary and wallaby skeletons used for comparison.

kangaroo, but with a number of bird-like attributes, just as Huxley's theory predicted.

Dollo proved to be tirelessly inventive in his approach to the fossil creatures that he described – he dissected crocodiles and birds in order to better understand the biology and detailed musculature of these animals and how it could be used to identify the soft tissues of his dinosaurs. In many respects, he was adopting a decidedly forensic approach to understanding those mysterious fossils. Dollo was regarded as the architect of a new style of palaeontology that became known as palaeobiology. Dollo demonstrated that palaeontology should be expanded to investigate the biology, and by implication ecology and behaviour, of these extinct creatures. His final contribution to the *Iguanodon* story was a paper he published in 1923 to honour the centenary of Mantell's original discoveries. He succinctly summarized his views on the dinosaur, identifying it as the dinosaurian ecological equivalent of the giraffe (or indeed Mantell's giant ground sloth). Dollo concluded that its posture enabled it to reach high into trees to gather its fodder, which it was able to draw into its mouth by using a long, muscular tongue; the sharp beak was used to nip off tough stems, while the characteristic teeth served to pulp the food before it was swallowed. So firmly was this authoritative interpretation adopted, based as it was on a set of complete articulated skeletons, that it stood, literally and metaphorically, unchallenged for the next 60 years. This was reinforced by the distribution of replica, mounted skeletons of *Iguanodon* from Brussels to many of the great museums around the world during the early years of the 20th century, and also by the many popular and influential textbooks written on the subject.

Dinosaur palaeontology in decline

Paradoxically, the culmination of Dollo's remarkable work on this dinosaur and his international recognition as the 'father' of the new palaeobiology in the 1920s marked the beginning of a serious decline in the perceived relevance of this area of research within the larger theatre of natural science.

In the interval between the mid-1920s and the mid-1960s, palaeontology, and particularly the study of dinosaurs, rather unexpectedly stagnated. The excitement of the early discoveries, notably those in Europe, was succeeded by more the spectacular 'bone wars' that gripped America during the last three decades of the 19th century. These centred on a furious – and sometimes violent – race to discover and name new dinosaurs, and had all the hallmarks of an academic equivalent of the 'Wild West'. At its centre were Edward Drinker Cope (a protégé of the polite and unassuming Professor Leidy) and his 'opponent' Othniel Charles Marsh at Yale University. They hired gangs of thugs to venture out into the American mid-West to collect as many new dinosaur bones as possible. This 'war' resulted in a frenzy of scientific publications naming dozens of new dinosaurs, many of whose names still resonate today, such as *Brontosaurus*, *Stegosaurus*, *Triceratops*, and *Diplodocus*.

Equally fascinating discoveries were made, partly by accident, during the early 20th century in exotic places such as Mongolia by Roy Chapman Andrews of the American Museum of Natural History in New York (the real-life hero/explorer upon whom was based the mythical 'Indiana Jones'); and in German East Africa (Tanzania) by Werner Janensch of the Berlin Museum of Natural History.

More new dinosaurs were continually being discovered and named from various places around the world, and although they created dramatic centrepieces in museums, palaeontologists seemed to be doing little more than adding new names to the roster of extinct creatures. A sense of failure took hold to the extent that some even used dinosaurs as examples of a theory of extinction based on 'racial senescence'. The general thesis was that they had lived for so long that their genetic constitution was simply exhausted and no longer capable of generating the novelty necessary for the group as a whole to survive. This supported the idea that dinosaurs were merely an experiment in animal design and evolution that the world had eventually passed by.

Not surprisingly, many biologists and theoreticians began to view this area of research with an increasingly jaundiced eye. New discoveries, though undeniably exciting, did not seem to be providing data that would lead in any particular direction. Discovery required the scientific formalities of description and naming of these creatures, but beyond that all interest seemed essentially museological: to be brutal, the work was seen as the equivalent of 'stamp collecting'. Dinosaurs, and many other fossil discoveries, offered glimpses of the tapestry of life within the fossil record, but beyond this their scientific value seemed questionable.

Several factors justified this change of perception: Gregor Mendel's work (published in 1866, but overlooked until 1900) on the laws of particulate inheritance (genetics) provided the crucial mechanism to support Darwin's theory of evolution by means of natural selection. Mendel's work was elegantly merged with Darwin's theory in order to create 'Neodarwinism' in the 1930s. At a stroke, Mendelian genetics solved one of Darwin's most fundamental worries about his theory: how favourable characteristics (genes or alleles in the new Mendelian language) could be passed from generation to generation. In the absence of any better understanding of the mechanism of inheritance in the mid-19th century, Darwin had assumed that characters or traits, the features subject to selection according to his theory, were blended when inherited by the next generation. This, however, was a fatal flaw, because Darwin realized that any favourable traits would simply be diluted out of existence if they were blended during reproduction from generation to generation. Neodarwinism clarified matters enormously, Mendelian genetics provided a degree of mathematical rigour to the theory, and the revitalized subject rapidly spawned new avenues of research. It led to the new sciences of genetics and molecular biology, culminating in Crick and Watson's model of DNA in 1953, as well as huge developments in the fields of behavioural evolution and evolutionary ecology.

Unfortunately, this fertile intellectual ground was not so obviously available to palaeontologists. Self-evidently, genetic mechanisms could not be studied in fossil creatures, so it seemed that they could offer no material evidence to the intellectual thrust of evolutionary studies during much of the remainder of the 20th century. Darwin had already foreseen the limitations of palaeontology in the context of his new theory. Using his inimitable reasoning, he noted the limited contribution that could be made by fossils to any of the debates concerning his new evolutionary theory. In a chapter of the *Origin of Species* devoted to the subject of the 'imperfections of the fossil record', Darwin noted that although fossils provided material proof of evolution during the history of life on Earth (harking back to the older progressionists' arguments), the geological succession of rocks, and the fossil record contained within in it, was lamentably incomplete. Comparing the geological record to a book charting the history of life on Earth, he wrote:

> . . . of this volume, only here and there a short chapter has been preserved; and of each page, only here and there a few lines.

> (Darwin, 1882, 6th edn.: 318)

Dinosaur palaeobiology: a new beginning

It was not until the 1960s and early 1970s that the study of fossils began to re-emerge as the subject of wider and more general interest. The catalyst for this re-awakening was a younger generation of evolutionarily minded scientists eager to demonstrate that the evidence from the fossil record was far from being a Darwinian 'closed book'. The premise that underpinned this new work was that while evolutionary biologists are obviously constrained by working with living animals in an essentially two-dimensional world – they are able to study species, but they do not witness the emergence of new species – palaeobiologists, by contrast, work in the third dimension of time. The fossil record provides sufficient time to allow new species to appear and others to become extinct. This permits palaeobiologists to pose questions that bear on the problems of evolution: does the geological timescale offer an added (or different) perspective on the process of evolution?; and, is the fossil record sufficiently informative that it can be teased apart to reveal some evolutionary secrets?

Detailed surveys of the geological record began to demonstrate rich successions of fossils (particularly shelled marine creatures) – considerably richer than Charles Darwin could ever have imagined, given the comparative infancy of palaeontological work in the middle of the 19th century. Out of this work emerged observations and theories that would challenge the views of biologists over the modes of biological evolution over long intervals of geological time. Sudden massive, worldwide extinction events and periods of faunal recovery were documented which could not have been predicted from Darwinian theory. Such events seemed to reset the evolutionary timetable of life in a virtual instant, and this prompted some theorists to take a much more 'episodic' or 'contingent' view of the history of life on Earth. Large-scale, or macroevolutionary, changes in global faunal diversity over time seemed to be demonstrable; these again were not predicted from Darwinian theory and required explanation.

Most notably, however, Niles Eldredge and Stephen Jay Gould proposed the theory of 'punctuated equilibrium'. They suggested that modern biological versions of evolutionary theory needed to be expanded, or modified, to accommodate patterns of change seen repeatedly among species in the fossil record. These consisted of prolonged periods of stasis (the 'equilibrium' period) during which relatively minor changes in species were observable, and contrasted with very short periods of rapid change (the 'punctuation'). These observations did not fit well with the Darwinian prediction of slow and progressive change in the appearance of species over time (dubbed 'evolutionary gradualism'). These ideas also prompted palaeobiologists to question the levels at which natural selection might function: perhaps it could operate above the level of the individual in some instances?

As a consequence, the whole field of palaeobiology became more dynamic, questioning, and also outward-looking; it was also prepared to integrate its work more broadly with other fields of science. Even highly influential evolutionary biologists such as John Maynard Smith, who had had little truck with fossils at all, were prepared to accept that palaeobiology had valuable contributions to make to the field.

While the general field of scientific palaeobiology was re-establishing its credentials, the mid-1960s was also a time of important new dinosaur discoveries; these were destined to spark ideas that are still important today. The epicentre of this renaissance was the Peabody Museum at Yale University, the original workplace of 'bone-fighter' Othniel Charles Marsh. However, this time it was in the person of John Ostrom, a young professor of palaeontology with a strong interest in dinosaurs.

Chapter 2
Dinosaur renaissance

The discovery of 'terrible claw'

In the summer of 1964 John Ostrom was prospecting for fossils
in Cretaceous rocks near Bridger, Montana, and collected the
fragmentary remains of a new and unusual predatory dinosaur.
Further collecting yielded more complete remains, and by 1969
Ostrom was able to describe the new dinosaur in sufficient detail
and to christen it *Deinonychus* ('terrible claw') in recognition of
a wickedly hooked, gaff-like claw on its hind foot.

Deinonychus (Figure 16) was a medium-sized (2–3 metres in
length), predatory dinosaur belonging to a group known as the
theropods. Ostrom noted a number of unexpected anatomical
features; these prepared the intellectual ground for a revolution
that would shatter the then rather firmly held view of dinosaurs
as archaic and outmoded creatures that plodded their way to
extinction at the close of the Mesozoic world.

However, Ostrom was far more interested in understanding the
biology of this puzzling animal than in simply listing its skeletal
features. This approach is far removed from the pejorative epithet
'stamp-collecting' that palaeontology had attracted, and echoes the
method of Louis Dollo in his earlier attempts to understand the
biology of the first complete *Iguanodon* skeletons (Chapter 1). As an

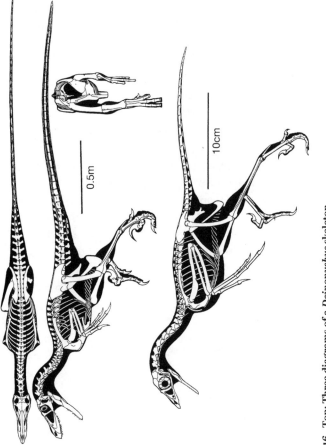

16. Top: Three diagrams of a *Deinonychus* skeleton.
Bottom: Diagram of *Archaeopteryx* with feathers removed to show its basic theropod affinity.

0.5m

10cm

Features of *Deinonychus*

i) The animal was clearly bipedal (it ran on its hind legs alone) and its legs were long and slender.

ii) Its feet were unusual in that of the three large toes on each, only two were designed to be walked upon, the inner toe was held clear of the ground and 'cocked' as if ready for action (a bit like a huge version of the sharp retractile claws in a cat's paw).

iii) The front part of the animal was counterbalanced at the hip by a long tail; however, this tail was not of the deep, muscular variety normally expected in these types of animal, but was flexible and muscled near the hips, becoming very narrow (almost pole-like) and stiffened by bundles of thin, bony rods along the rest of its length.

iv) The chest was short and compact, and supported very long arms that ended in sharply clawed (raptorial) three-fingered hands that swivelled on wrists that allowed the hands to be swung in a raking arc (like those of a praying mantis).

v) The neck was slender and curved (rather like that of a goose), but supported a very large head, which was equipped with long jaws, lined with sharp, curved, and saw-edged teeth; very large eye sockets that seem to point forward; and a much larger than expected braincase.

approach, it has more in common with modern forensic pathology, driven as it is by a need to assemble broad ranges of facts from a number of different scientific areas in order to arrive at rigorous interpretation, or hypothesis, on the basis of the available evidence; this is one of several driving forces behind today's palaeobiology.

Deducing the biology and natural history of *Deinonychus*

Looking at *Deinonychus* using this type of 'forensic' perspective, what do these features tell us about the animal and its way of life?

The jaws and teeth (sharp, with curved and serrated edges) confirm that this was a predator capable of slicing up and swallowing its prey. The eyes were large, pointed forward, and would have offered a degree of stereoscopic vision, which would be ideal for judging distance accurately: very useful for catching fast-moving prey, as well as for monitoring athletic movements in three-dimensional space. This serves, in part at least, to explain the relatively large brain (implied from its large braincase): the optic lobes would need to be large to process lots of complex visual information so that the animal could respond quickly, and the motor areas of the brain would need to be large and elaborate to process the higher-brain commands and then coordinate the rapid muscular responses of the body.

The need for an elaborate brain is further emphasized by considering the light stature and slender proportions of its legs, which are similar to those of modern, fast-moving animals and suggest that *Deinonychus* was a sprinter. The narrowness of each foot (just two walking toes, rather than the more stable, and more usual, 'tripod' effect of three) suggests that its sense of balance must have been particularly well developed; this is further supported by the fact that this animal was bipedal, and clearly able to walk while balanced on two feet alone (a feat that, as toddlers prove daily, needs to be learned and perfected through feedback between the brain and musculoskeletal system).

Linked to this issue of balance and coordination, the 'terrible claw' on each foot was clearly an offensive weapon, evidence of the animal's predatory lifestyle. But how, exactly, would it have been used? Two possibilities spring to mind: either it was capable of slashing at its prey with one foot at a time, as some large ground-dwelling birds such as ostriches and cassowaries do today (this implies that it could have balanced on one foot from time to time); alternatively, it may have attacked its prey using a two-footed kick, by jumping on its prey or by grasping its prey in its arms and giving a murderous double-kick – this latter style of fighting is employed by kangaroos when fighting rivals. We are unlikely to be able to decide which of these speculations might be nearest the truth.

The long arms and sharply clawed hands would be effective grapples for holding and ripping its prey in either of these prey-capture scenarios and the curious raking motion made possible by the wrist joints enhances their raptorial abilities considerably. In addition, the long, whip-like tail may well have served as a cantilever – the equivalent of a tightrope walker's pole to aid balance when slashing with one foot – or it could have served as a dynamic stabilizer, which would prove useful when chasing fast-moving prey that were capable of changing direction very quickly or when leaping on prey.

While this is not an exhaustive analysis of *Deinonychus* as a living creature, it does provide an outline of some of the reasoning that led Ostrom to conclude that *Deinonychus* was an athletic, surprisingly well-coordinated, and probably intelligent predatory dinosaur. Why should the discovery of this creature be regarded as so important to the field of dinosaur palaeobiology? To answer that question, it is necessary to take a broader view of the dinosaurs as a whole.

The traditional view of dinosaurs

Throughout the earlier part of the 20th century, it was widely (and perfectly reasonably) assumed that dinosaurs were a group of extinct reptiles. Admittedly, some were dramatically large or rather outlandish-looking compared to modern reptiles, but they were crucially still reptiles. Richard Owen (and Georges Cuvier before him) had confirmed that dinosaurs were anatomically most similar to living reptiles, creatures such as lizards and crocodiles. On this basis it was inferred, logically, that most of their biological attributes would have been similar, if not identical, to those of these living reptiles: they laid shelled eggs, had scaly skins, and had a 'cold-blooded', or ectothermic, physiology.

To help demonstrate that this view was correct, Roy Chapman Andrews had discovered that Mongolian dinosaurs laid shelled eggs, and Louis Dollo (among others) had identified impressions of their scaly skins; so their overall physiology would be expected to resemble that of living reptiles. This combination of attributes created an entirely unexceptional view of dinosaurs: they were large, scaly, but crucially slow-witted and sluggish creatures. Their habits were assumed to be similar to those of lizards, snakes, and crocodiles, which most biologists had only ever seen in zoos. The only puzzle was that dinosaurs were mostly built on a far grander scale compared to even the very biggest of known crocodiles.

There were many depictions of dinosaurs in popular books, and scientific ones, wallowing in swamps, or squatting as if barely able to support their gargantuan bodies. Some particularly memorable examples, such as O. C. Marsh's *Stegosaurus* and *Brontosaurus*, reinforced these conceptions. Both had enormous bodies and the tiniest of brains (even Marsh remarked in disbelief at the 'walnut-sized' brain cavity of his *Stegosaurus*). So lacking in brainpower was *Stegosaurus* that it was deemed necessary to invent a 'second brain', in its hip region, to act as a sort of back-up or relay station for information from distant parts of its body, thus confirming the 'stupid' and 'lowly' status of dinosaurs beyond reasonable doubt.

While the weight of comparative evidence undoubtedly sustained this particular perception of the dinosaur, it ignored, or simply glossed over, contradictory observations: many dinosaurs, such as little *Compsognathus* (Figure 14), were known to be lightly built and designed for rapid movement. By implication they should have had rather un-reptile-like levels of activity.

Armed with this battery of prevailing opinion and Ostrom's observations and interpretations based on *Deinonychus*, it is easier to appreciate how this creature must have been challenging his mind. *Deinonychus* was a relatively large-brained, fast-moving predator capable of sprinting on its hind legs and attacking its prey – common sense said that this was no ordinary reptile.

One of Ostrom's students, Robert Bakker, took up this theme by aggressively challenging the view that dinosaurs were dull, stupid creatures. Bakker argued that there was compelling evidence that dinosaurs were more similar to today's mammals and birds. It should not be forgotten that this argument echoes the incredibly far-sighted comments made by Richard Owen in 1842, when he first conceived the idea of the dinosaur. Mammals and birds are regarded as 'special' because they can maintain high activity levels that are attributed to their 'warm-blooded', or endothermic, physiology. Living endotherms maintain a high and constant body temperature, have highly efficient lungs to maintain sustained aerobic activity levels, are capable of being highly active whatever the ambient temperature, and are able to maintain large and sophisticated brains; all these attributes distinguish birds and mammals from the other vertebrates on Earth.

The range of evidence Bakker used is interesting when considered from our now slightly more 'tuned' palaeobiological perspective. Using the anatomical observations made by Ostrom, he argued, in agreement with Owen before him, that:

i)   Dinosaurs had legs arranged pillar-like beneath the body (as do mammals and birds), rather than legs that sprawl out sideways from the body, as seen in lizards and crocodiles.

ii) Some dinosaurs had complex, bird-like lungs, which would have permitted them to breathe more efficiently – as would be necessary for a highly energetic creature.

iii) Dinosaurs could, based on the proportions of their limbs, run at speed (unlike lizards and crocodiles).

However, borrowing from the fields of histology, pathology, and microscopy, Bakker reported that thin sections of dinosaur bone, when viewed under a microscope, showed evidence of a complex structure and rich blood supply that would have allowed a rapid turnover of vital minerals between bone and blood plasma – exactly paralleling that seen in modern mammals.

Turning to the field of ecology, Bakker analysed the relative abundances of predators and their supposed prey among samples of fossils representing time-averaged communities from the fossil record and the present day. By comparing modern communities of endotherms (cats) and ectotherms (predatory lizards), he estimated that endotherms consume, on average, ten times the volume of prey during the same time interval. When he surveyed ancient (Permian) communities, by counting fossils of this age in museum collections, he observed rather similar numbers of potential predators and prey. When he examined some dinosaur communities from the Cretaceous period, he noticed that there was a considerably larger number of potential prey compared to the number of predators. He came to a similar conclusion after studying Tertiary mammal communities.

Using these admittedly simple proxies, he suggested that dinosaurs (or at least the predators) must have had metabolic requirements more similar to mammals; for the communities to stay in some degree of balance, there needed to be sufficient prey items to support the appetites of the predators.

Within the fields of geology and the 'new' palaeobiology, he also looked for macroevolutionary evidence (large-scale patterns of change in fossil abundance) taken from the fossil record. Bakker examined the times of origin and extinction of the dinosaurs for evidence that might have had a bearing on their putative physiology. The time of origin of the dinosaurs, during the Late Triassic (225 Ma), coincided with the time of the evolution of some of the most mammal-like creatures, with the first true mammals appearing about 200 Ma. Bakker suggested that dinosaurs evolved into a successful group simply because they developed an endothermic metabolism slightly earlier than mammals. If not, or so he argued, dinosaurs would never have been able to compete with the first truly endothermic mammals. In further support of this idea, he noted that true early mammals were small, probably nocturnal insectivores and scavengers during the entirety of the Mesozoic, when the dinosaurs ruled on land, and only diversified into the bewildering variety that we know today once the dinosaurs became extinct at the end of the Cretaceous. On that basis, so Bakker argued, dinosaurs simply *had* to be endotherms, otherwise the supposedly 'superior' endothermic mammals would have conquered the land and replaced the dinosaurs in the Early Jurassic. Moreover, when he considered the time of extinction of the dinosaurs at the close of the Cretaceous (65 Ma), Bakker believed that there was evidence that the world had been subjected to a temporary period of low global temperatures. Since dinosaurs were, in his opinion, large, endothermic, and 'naked' (that is, they were scale-covered and had neither hair nor feathers to keep their bodies warm), they were unable to survive a period of rapid climatic cooling and therefore died out. This left the mammals and birds to survive to the present day. Dinosaurs were too big to shelter in burrows, as do the modern reptiles that evidently survived the Cretaceous catastrophe.

Combining all these lines of argument, Bakker was able to propose that far from being slow and dull, dinosaurs were intelligent, highly active creatures that had stolen the world from the traditionally superior mammals for the remaining 160 million years of the Mesozoic. Rather than being ousted from the world by the evolutionary rise of superior mammals, they had only given up their dominance because of some freakish climatic event 65 million years ago.

It should now be obvious that the palaeobiological agenda for research is rather more intellectually broad-based. The 'expert' can no longer rely upon specialist knowledge in his or her own narrow area of expertise. However, this part of the story does not end here. John Ostrom had another important part to play in this saga.

Ostrom and *Archaeopteryx*: the earliest bird

Having described *Deinonychus*, Ostrom continued to investigate the biological properties of dinosaurs. In the early 1970s a trifling discovery in a museum in Germany was to bring him right back to the centre of some heated discussions. While examining collections of flying reptiles, Ostrom noticed one specimen, collected from a quarry in Bavaria, that did not belong to a pterosaur, or flying reptile, as its label suggested. It was a section of a leg including the thigh, knee-joint, and shin. Its detailed anatomical shape reminded Ostrom of that of *Deinonychus*. On closer inspection, he could also make out the faintest impressions of feathers! This was clearly an unrecognized specimen of the fabled early bird *Archaeopteryx* (Figure 13). Excited by his new discovery, and naturally puzzled by its apparent similarity to *Deinonychus*, Ostrom began carefully restudying all the known *Archaeopteryx* specimens.

The more Ostrom studied *Archaeopteryx*, the more convinced he became of the extent of the anatomical similarity between this creature and his much larger predatory dinosaur *Deinonychus* (Figure 16). This led him to reassess the monumental and then authoritative work on bird origins that had been written by ornithologist and anatomist Gerhard Heilmann in 1926. The sheer number of anatomical similarities between carnivorous theropod dinosaurs and early birds drove Ostrom to question Heilmann's conclusion in that work that the similarities could only have been due to evolutionary convergence.

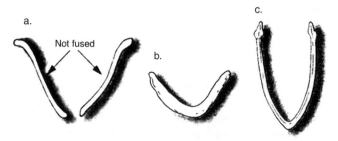

17. Comparison of the clavicles of (a) early theropod dinosaurs, (b) *Archaeopteryx* (clavicles are fused together), and (c) modern birds

Armed with more recent discoveries of dinosaurs around the world, Ostrom was able to show that a number of dinosaurs did actually possess small clavicles, removing at a stroke Heilmann's big stumbling block to a dinosaurian ancestry for birds. Encouraged by this discovery and his own detailed observations on theropods and *Archaeopteryx*, Ostrom launched a comprehensive assault on Heilmann's theory in a series of articles in the early 1970s. This led to the gradual acceptance of a theropod dinosaur ancestry of birds by the great majority of palaeontologists, and would no doubt have pleased the far-sighted Huxley and deeply irritated Owen.

The close anatomical, and therefore biological, similarity between theropods and the earliest birds added fuel to the controversy concerning the metabolic status of dinosaurs. Birds are highly active, endothermic creatures; perhaps the theropod dinosaurs might also have possessed an elevated metabolism. The once clear dividing line between feathered birds, with their distinctive anatomy and biology which merited them being separated off from all other vertebrates as a discrete class, the Aves, and other more typical members of the class Reptilia (of which the dinosaurs were just one extinct group) became worryingly blurred. The extent of this blurred line has become even more pronounced in recent years (as we shall see in Chapter 6).

Chapter 3
New light on *Iguanodon*

The resurgence in palaeobiology in the 1960s, and the new insights into dinosaurs prompted by John Ostrom's important work, provided a spur to reinvestigate some of the earliest discoveries.

Louis Dollo's description of the incredible discoveries of *Iguanodon* at Bernissart created the image of a giant (5 metres tall, 11 metres long) kangaroo-like creature. It had:

> powerful back legs and a massive tail that helped it to balance . . . [and] was a plant eater . . . it grasped bunches of leaves with its long tongue, then pulled them into its mouth to be clipped off with the beak.

The picture of *Iguanodon* was of an animal that was the dinosaur equivalent of a 'tree browser', represented in the recent past by the giant South American ground sloths and today by giraffes. Dollo himself referred to *Iguanodon* as a 'girafe reptilienne'. Rather surprisingly, nearly every aspect of this vision of *Iguanodon* is incorrect or seriously misleading.

Bernissart: a ravine where *Iguanodon* perished?

Some of the earliest work at Bernissart focused on the extraordinary circumstances of the original discovery. The dinosaurs had been unearthed in a coal mine at depths of between 356 and 322 metres below the surface (Figure 18). This was unexpected, as the coal seams being excavated were known to be Palaeozoic in age and dinosaurs are of course unknown in rocks of such antiquity. However, the *Iguanodon* skeletons were not found in the coal seams themselves, but in a pocket of shale of Cretaceous age that cut across the more ancient coal-bearing rocks. Mining geologists had a commercial interest in discovering the extent of these clays, and the degree to which they might affect coal extraction, so they began mapping the area.

Cross sections of the mine, created during these geological investigations, suggested that the horizontal layers of Palaeozoic rocks (with their valuable coal seams) were occasionally cut through very steeply by beds of Mesozoic shale (finely laminated clays). The cross sections gave the first impression of steep-sided ravines cut into the ancient rocks, and formed the basis for a graphic and rather appealing notion that the Bernissart dinosaurs represented a herd that had tumbled to their deaths (Figure 18). Dollo, himself no geologist, was more inclined to the idea that these dinosaurs had lived, and died, in a narrow gorge. However, the more dramatic story had the greater impact, and was further embellished by suggestions that they had been stampeded into the ravine by huge predatory dinosaurs (megalosaurs), or by some freak event such as a forest fire. This was not entirely wishful thinking: extremely rare fragments of a large predatory dinosaur were discovered within the *Iguanodon*-bearing beds; and charcoal-like lumps of coal were recovered from some of the rubble-like deposits found in the region between the coal-bearing rocks and the dinosaur-bearing shaly beds.

The discoveries at Bernissart presented a huge logistic challenge in the 1870s and early 1880s. Complete skeletons of dinosaurs measuring up to 11 metres in length had been discovered at the bottom of a deep mine; they were the focus of worldwide interest at the time, but how were they to be excavated and studied?

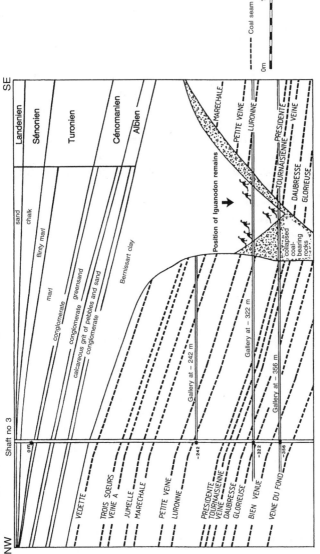

NW — SE

Shaft no 3

Landenien
Sénonien
Turonien
Cénomanien
Albien

sand
chalk
flinty marl
marl
conglomerate
conglomerate greensand
calcareous grit of pebbles and sand
conglomerate
conglomerate

Bernissart clay

Position of Iguanodon remains

Gallery at – 242 m
Gallery at – 322 m
Gallery at – 356 m

collapsed coal-bearing rocks

VEDETTE
TROIS SŒURS
VEINE A
JUMELLE
MARECHALE
PETITE VEINE
LURONNE
PRESIDENTE
TOURNAISIENNE
VEINE
DAUBRESSE
GLORIEUSE
BIEN VENUE
VEINE DU FOND

MARECHALE
PETITE VEINE
LURONNE
TOURNAISIENNE
PRESIDENTE
DAUBRESSE
GLORIEUSE
VEINE

0m
–242
–322
–356

0m   100m
– – – Coal seam

18. **Geological section of the Bernissart mine**

A cooperative venture was arranged between the Belgian government, funding the scientists and technicians of the Royal Natural History Museum in Brussels, and the miners and engineers at the colliery in Bernissart. Each skeleton was carefully exposed and its position in the mine recorded systematically on plan diagrams. Every skeleton was divided into manageable blocks approximately 1 metre square. Each block, protected by a jacket of plaster of Paris, was carefully numbered and recorded on plan drawings (Figure 19) before being lifted and transported to Brussels.

Back in Brussels, the blocks were reassembled from the records, rather like a gigantic jigsaw puzzle. The plaster was painstakingly removed to reveal the bones of each skeleton. At this point an artist, Gustave Lavalette, specially commissioned for the project, drew the skeleton in its death pose before any further preparation or extraction was undertaken (Figure 20). Some skeletons were completely extracted from the shale and mounted to create a

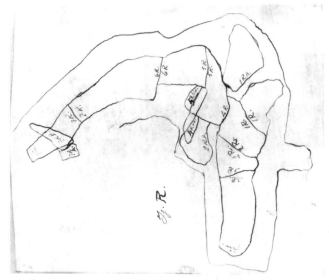

19. Plan diagram of an excavated *Iguanodon* skeleton from Bernissart

magnificent display that can be seen to this day at the (renamed) Royal Institute of Natural Sciences, in Parc Léopold, Brussels. Other skeletons were cleared of the shale matrix on one side only and arranged in their burial pose on wooden scaffolding supporting vast banks of plaster. This display mimics their entombed positions when they were first discovered in the mine at Bernissart.

The original plans of each excavation, and some crude geological sections and sketches of the discoveries, are preserved in the archives of the Royal Institute in Brussels. This information has been 'mined', this time for clues concerning the geological nature of the dinosaur burial site.

The geology of the coal-mining area of the Mons Basin, in which lies the village of Bernissart, had been the subject of study before dinosaurs were ever discovered. A major review in 1870 pointed out

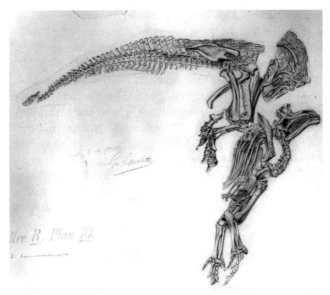

20. Lavalette's drawing of the *Iguanodon* skeleton seen in Figure 19

that the coal-bearing strata of the Mons Basin were pock-marked by 'cran' (naturally formed subterranean pits). Each 'cran' was of limited extent and filled with shales. It was concluded that these had formed by the dissolution of Palaeozoic rocks deep underground. The roofs of such caverns collapse periodically under the sheer weight of the overlying rocks, so the spaces become filled with whatever lies above: in this case soft clays or shales. The collapse of such sediments had been recorded locally in the Mons area as rather alarming, earthquake-like shocks. By amazing coincidence, a minor 'earthquake' of this type took place while the dinosaurs were being excavated in August 1878 at Bernissart. Minor collapses in the galleries were noted, as well as flooding, but the miners and scientists were soon able to resume their work once the flood water had been pumped out.

Despite all the local geological knowledge, it is very curious that the scientists from the Museum in Brussels incorrectly interpreted the geological nature of the 'cran' at Bernissart. The mining engineers produced crude geological sections from the tunnels that yielded the dinosaurs. These showed that immediately beyond the coal-bearing seams there was a section of 10–11 metres of breccia (broken beds containing irregular blocks of limestone and coal mixed with silt and clay, the 'collapsed coal-bearing rocks' of Figure 18) before entering steeply dipping, but more regularly stratified, shales that yielded the fossils. Toward the middle of the 'cran' the clay beds were horizontally bedded, and as the tunnel approached the opposite side of the 'cran' the beds once again became steeply tilted in the opposite direction before passing again into a brecciated region and finally re-entering the coal-bearing deposits. The symmetry of the geology across the 'cran' is exactly what would be expected if overlying sediments had slumped into a large cavity.

The sediments in which the dinosaurs are embedded also directly contradict the ravine or river-valley interpretations. Finely stratified shales containing the fossils are normally deposited in low-energy, relatively shallow-water environments, probably equivalent to a large lake or lagoon. There is simply no evidence for catastrophic deaths caused by herds of animals plunging into a ravine. In fact, the dinosaur skeletons were found in separate layers of sediment (along with fish, crocodiles, turtles, thousands of leaf impressions, and even rare insect fragments), proving that they definitely did not all die at the same time and therefore could never have been part of a single herd of animals.

Study of the orientation of the fossil skeletons within the mine suggests that dinosaur carcasses were washed into the burial area on separate occasions and from different directions. It was as if the direction of flow of the river that carried their carcasses had changed from time to time, exactly as happens in large, slow-moving river systems today.

So, as early as the 1870s, it was clearly understood that there were neither 'ravines' nor 'river valleys' in which the dinosaurs at Bernissart might have perished. It is fascinating how the dramatic discovery of dinosaurs at Bernissart seems to have demanded an equally dramatic explanation for their deaths, and that such fantasies were uncritically adopted even though they flew in the face of the scientific evidence available at the time.

The image of *Iguanodon* as a gigantic kangaroo-style creature has become iconic because of the generous distribution of full-sized skeletal casts to many museums around the world. But does the evidence for this restoration survive further scrutiny?

A 'twist' in the tail

Re-examining the skeletal evidence from first principles, the anatomy of the skeletons from Bernissart reveal some disconcerting features. One of the most obvious concerns the massive tail of *Iguanodon*. The well-known reconstruction shows the animal (Figure 12) propped, in true kangaroo style, using its tail and hind legs tripod-like. To adopt this posture, the tail curves upward to the hip. In sharp contrast, all the documentary and fossil evidence points to this animal normally holding its tail essentially straight or somewhat downwardly curved. This is clearly seen in the specimens arranged on banks of plaster in the museum, and in the wonderful pencil sketches made of their skeletons before they were exhibited (Figure 20). It could of course be argued that this shape was simply an artefact of preservation, but this explanation is definitely not plausible here. The backbone was in effect 'trussed' on either side by a trellis-like arrangement of long bony tendons that held the backbone quite deliberately straight; these can be seen in Figure 20. As a result, the heavy, muscled tail served as an enormous cantilever to balance the weight of the front part of the body at the hips. The truth is that the upward sweep of the tail seen in Dollo's reconstructions would have been physically impossible for these animals in life. Careful examination of the skeleton revealed that the tail was deliberately broken in several places to achieve the upward bend – a case perhaps of Louis Dollo making the skeleton fit his personal ideas a little over-zealously.

This discovery disturbs the pose of the remainder of the skeleton. If the tail is straightened so that it can adopt a more 'natural' shape, then the tilt of the body changes dramatically, with the backbone becoming more horizontal and balanced at the hip. As a result the chest is lower, bringing the arms and hands closer to the ground and raising questions about their likely function.

Hands or feet?

The hand of *Iguanodon* has become part of dinosaurian folklore for one obvious reason. The conical thumb-spike was originally identified as a rhinoceros-like horn on the nose of the *Iguanodon* (Figure 9) and was immortalized in the giant concrete models erected at London's Crystal Palace (Figure 2, Chapter 1). It was not until Dollo provided the first definitive reconstruction of *Iguanodon* in 1882 that it was proved to everyone's satisfaction that this bone was indeed a part of the dinosaur's hand. However, the hand (and the entire forelimb) of this dinosaur held a few more surprises.

The thumb, or first finger, comprises a large, conical, claw-bearing bone that sticks up at right angles to the rest of the hand and can be moved very little (Figure 21A). The second, third, and fourth fingers are very differently arranged: three long bones (metacarpals) form the palm of the hand and are bound tightly together by strong ligaments; the fingers are jointed to the ends of these metacarpals and are short, stubby, and end in flattened and blunt hooves. When these bones were manipulated, to see what their true range of movement was likely to be, it was found that the fingers splayed outwards (away from each other) and certainly could not flex to form a fist and perform simple grasping functions, as might have been expected. This distinctive arrangement looks similar to that seen in the *feet* of this animal: the three central toes of each foot are similarly shaped and jointed, splay apart, and end in flattened hooves. The fifth finger is different from all the others: it is quite separate from the previous four and set at a wide angle from the remainder of the hand; it is also long and has a wide range of movement at each joint, and was presumably unusually flexible.

This re-examination led me to dramatically revise earlier ideas and conclude that the hand is one of the most peculiar seen in the entire animal kingdom. The thumb was without doubt an impressive, stiletto-like weapon of defence (Figure 21B); the three central fingers were clearly adapted to bear weight (rather than for grasping things as hands usually do); and the fifth finger was sufficiently long and flexible to act as a truly finger-like grasping (prehensile) organ (Figure 21A).

The idea that the hand could act as a foot for walking upon, or at least supporting some of the body weight, was revolutionary – but was it true? This prompted further research on the arm and shoulder for additional evidence that might confirm such a radical reinterpretation.

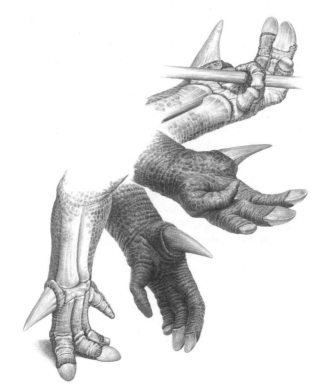

21A. *Iguanodon*'s hand, showing a range of uses

First of all, the wrist proved to be interesting. The bones of the wrist are welded together to form a bony block, instead of being a row of smooth, rounded bones that could slide past one another in order to allow that hand to swivel against the forearm. All the individual wrist bones have been welded together by bony cement, and are further strengthened around the outside by strands of bony ligament. These features obviously combined to lock the wrist firmly against the hand and forearm bones and resist the forces acting through them during weight-bearing, as would be necessary if the hands were truly acting as feet.

21B. The stiletto-like thumb of *Iguanodon* in action

The remainder of the arm bones are extremely stoutly built, again primarily for strength during weight support, rather than for allowing flexibility as is more normal with genuine arms. The stiffness of the forearm has important consequences for the way in which the hand would have been placed on the ground – the fingers would have pointed outward and the palms inward – an unusual consequence of converting a hand into a foot. The pose of the hand, in this rather awkward manner, has been confirmed by examination of the shape of forefoot prints left by this dinosaur.

The upper arm (humerus) is massive, rather pillar-like, and shows evidence that it anchored huge arm and shoulder muscles. This is

22. New reconstruction of *Iguanodon*

also unusually long, over three-quarters the length of the hind limb. The true size of the arms is somewhat masked in the original skeletal reconstructions, because they were folded against the chest and always *seemed* shorter than they really are.

Finally, the shoulder bones are large and powerfully built, which makes perfect sense if the arms are functioning as legs. But the shoulders show another unexpected feature. In the centre of the chest of the larger skeletons at Bernissart there is an irregular bone that grew in the soft tissues across the centre of the chest between the shoulder joints. This bone is pathological in origin – it formed as a response to strain within the chest created while the animal was walking on all fours (and is called an intersternal ossification).

Reassessing the posture of *Iguanodon* in the light of these observations, it seems clear that a more natural pose of the backbone was horizontal, with the body weight distributed along the backbone and largely balanced at the hips and supported by the massive and strong hind legs. The ossified tendons distributed along the spine, above the chest, hip, and tail, clearly acted as tensioners to distribute body weight along the backbone. This pose allowed the front limbs to reach the ground, and these were used for weight support while these animals were stationary. *Iguanodon* probably moved slowly on all fours at least part of the time (Figure 22).

Size and sex

The Bernissart discoveries are notable for comprising two types of *Iguanodon*. One (*Iguanodon bernissartensis* – quite literally 'the *Iguanodon* that lived in Bernissart') is large and robustly built, and represented by more than 35 skeletons; the other (*Iguanodon atherfieldensis*, formerly called *I. mantelli* – literally 'Mantell's *Iguanodon*') is smaller and more delicately built (approximately 6 metres in length) and represented by only two skeletons.

These specimens were regarded as distinct species until they were reassessed in the 1920s, by Francis Baron Nopcsa, a nobleman from Transylvania and a palaeontologist. The discovery of two quite similar types of dinosaur that evidently lived in the same place, at the same time, prompted him to ask the simple and yet obvious question: are they males and females of the same species? Nopcsa attempted to determine sexual differences in a number of fossil species. In the case of the *Iguanodon* from Bernissart he concluded that the smaller and rarer species was the male and the larger and more numerous species was the female. He observed, perfectly reasonably, that it is often the case that female reptiles are larger than males. The biological reason for this is that females often have to grow large numbers of thick-shelled eggs; these drain considerable resources from the body before they are laid.

While this seems quite a reasonable supposition, it is in fact very difficult to prove scientifically. Apart from size, which is surprisingly variable among reptiles as a whole and not nearly as consistent a feature as Nopcsa would have had us believe, the features used to distinguish the sexes among living reptiles are most commonly found in the soft anatomy of the sex organs themselves, coloration of the skin, or behaviour. This is particularly unfortunate because only very rarely do fossils ever preserve such features.

The most valuable evidence would be the discovery of soft anatomical fossils of the sexual organs of *Iguanodon* – unfortunately, this is an extremely unlikely event. And, since we can never know their true biology and behaviour, we have to be a little cautious and also realistic. For the present, it is safer to record the differences (we may have our own suspicions, perhaps), but simply leave it at that.

A careful study of the more abundant large *Iguanodon* from Bernissart revealed that a few were smaller than the average.

Measuring the proportions of each of these skeletons revealed an unexpected growth change. Smaller, presumably immature specimens had shorter arms than would have been expected. The comparatively short-armed juveniles may well have been more adept bipedal runners, but as large adult size and stature was achieved they may have become progressively more accustomed to moving around on all fours. This also fits with the observation of an intersternal ossification in only larger, presumably adult, individuals, which spent more of their time on all fours compared to smaller, younger individuals.

Soft tissues

Soft tissues of fossil creatures are preserved only rarely, and under exceptional preservational conditions, so palaeontologists have developed techniques to decipher clues concerning this type of biology of dinosaurs both directly and indirectly.

Louis Dollo reported small patches of skin impression on parts of the skeletons of *Iguanodon*. A number of the skeletons from Bernissart are shown in a classic 'death pose' with the powerful neck muscles contracted, during *rigor mortis*, pulling the neck into a sharp curve and turning the head upward and backward. That this pose has been maintained during the time between death and eventual burial implies that the carcass of the animal had stiffened and dried out. Under such conditions, its tough, parchment-like skin would have formed a rigid surface against which the fine-grained muds would have moulded themselves during burial. Provided that the entombing sediment compacted sufficiently to retain their shape, prior to the inevitable rotting and disappearance of the dinosaur's organic tissues, then (as with simple clay moulds) an impression of the texture of the skin surface would have been preserved in the sediment.

In the case of *Iguanodon* the texture of the skin impression that was

23. *Iguanodon* skin impression

preserved confirmed expectations: it shows a finely scaled, flexible covering, very similar in appearance to that seen on the skin of modern lizards (Figure 23). Clearly, the disappearance of the original tissue means that any traces of skin pigments have long vanished.

In addition to the detailed work that has to be done simply to describe the bones of the dinosaur's skeleton, it is also possible to focus on certain parts of the body, notably the hips, shoulders, and head, for clues concerning the arrangement of its muscles. The reason for this is that at the places where muscles and tendons attach to the surface of bones, tell-tale surface markings such as elevated ridges of bone or distinctively pitted muscle scars often form. Skeletal bone is a surprisingly plastic material. Bones must change shape as the body grows, or if it has to repair itself following trauma such as a fracture. What may be less obvious is that even when the body is full grown, its bones continue to be remodelled in response to ever-changing patterns of stress and strain. For example, an individual taking up a course of weight-training will deposit extra skeletal bone in order to cope with the increased load, especially if this training regime is continued over time.

In particular areas of the body, where large muscles exert forces on the skeleton, the scarring on bones can be quite distinctive, even in fossils; this creates a crude map that allows some of the original musculature to be reconstructed (Figure 24). Such reconstructions are based on the known muscular arrangements seen in related living animals, tempered by allowances for the anatomical differences or novelties seen in the fossil animal that is being investigated.

Although far from scientifically ideal, an example of this kind of approach when trying to understand the musculature of *Iguanodon* is to use as a starting point information from two of the nearest living relatives of dinosaurs: birds and crocodiles. Clearly neither of

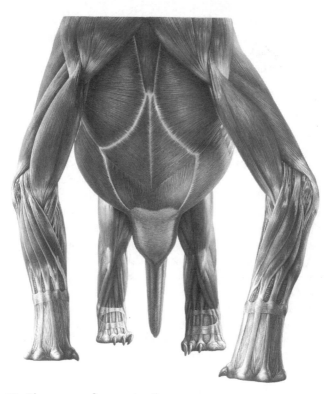

24. Dinosaur muscle reconstruction

these types of animal represent, at all accurately, the anatomy of *Iguanodon*: birds are highly modified for flight, have no teeth, have a minuscule tail and unusually modified hips and leg muscles; crocodiles, though more conventionally reptilian in shape, are highly specialized as aquatic predators. Despite these real problems, they provide a general framework or template – termed the 'extant phylogenetic bracket', or EPB – for reconstruction that can be supplemented by the finer details of the anatomy of *Iguanodon*.

The latter includes the general evidence from the overall physical

The extant phylogenetic bracket (EPB)

By creating a phylogenetic tree of the nearest relatives of dinosaurs, it is clear that crocodiles evolved *before* dinosaurs appeared and that birds evolved *after* the earliest dinosaurs. Dinosaurs are therefore sandwiched evolutionarily between living crocodiles and living birds.

Anatomical features shared by both living birds and crocodiles should also be present in dinosaurs because they are quite literally 'bracketed' by these living creatures. Sometimes this type of approach can help to deduce biological features among extinct groups even when there is no clear physical evidence for such features. However, given how specialized creatures such as dinosaurs can be, when compared to living crocodiles and birds, this approach must be used cautiously.

design (shape and arrangement of the bones) of the skeleton or skull, and the influence that these would have on the distribution and functioning of the muscles. Such reconstructions also need to account for such factors as the proposed method of locomotion. For example, the details of the joints between the limb bones, a consideration of the simple mechanics associated with the positioning and range of movement of the limbs that was possible at each limb joint; and, in some cases, the real evidence left behind by dinosaurs in the form of fossilized tracks that indicate how they really did move around when alive.

While examining many bony fragments of *Iguanodon* in the collections of the Natural History Museum in London, an unusual specimen caught my eye. It consisted of the battered remains of a

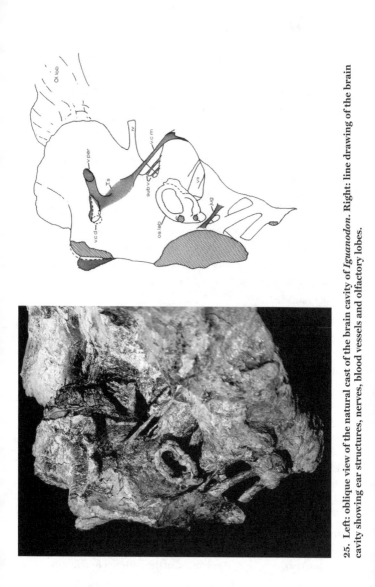

25. **Left: oblique view of the natural cast of the brain cavity of *Iguanodon*. Right: line drawing of the brain cavity showing ear structures, nerves, blood vessels and olfactory lobes.**

large, partial skull. A few teeth exposed in its upper jaw betrayed that it was indeed *Iguanodon*, but beyond that it seemed useless anatomically. For interest's sake, I decided to cut the specimen in half to see if any of its internal anatomy was better preserved. What was revealed proved to be unexpectedly interesting and exciting. Although the bones were battered and eroded, it was clear that this skull had been buried in soft, silty mud that had seeped into all the spaces. The mud had hardened (lithified) to a concrete-like consistency over millions of years. The lithification process was so complete that the mudstone had become impermeable so that ground-water containing minerals was unable to seep through the rock and mineralize the skull bones; as a result the bones were relatively soft and crumbly.

This peculiar preservation offered an unusual opportunity to explore skull anatomy. Careful removal of the crumbly skull bones (rather than the hard mudstone matrix) revealed the shape of the internal spaces in the skull as a natural mudstone cast (Figure 25). It included the cavity where the brain had lain, the passages for the inner ear, and many of the blood vessels and nerve tracts that led to and from the brain cavity. Given that this particular animal had died approximately 130 million years ago, it does seem remarkable that it should prove possible to reconstruct so much of its soft anatomy.

Iguanodon and dietary adaptation

The first recognizable fossils of *Iguanodon* were teeth, whose tell-tale features showed that it was a herbivorous animal; they were chisel-shaped to be able to slice and crush plants in the mouth before they were swallowed.

The need to cut and crush plant food hints at some important considerations concerning the diets of extinct creatures and some of the clues that their skeletons may contain.

Iguanodon's brain

The structure of the brain cavity shows large olfactory lobes at the front, suggesting that *Iguanodon* had a well-developed sense of smell. Large optic nerves passed through the braincase in the direction of the big eye sockets, apparently confirming that these animals had good vision. The large cerebral lobes indicate a well coordinated and active animal. The inner ear cast shows the looped semicircular canals that provided the animal's sense of balance, and a finger-like structure that was part of its hearing system. Beneath the brain cavity hangs a pod-like structure that housed the pituitary gland, which was responsible for regulating its hormone functions. Down either side of the cast are seen a series of large tubes, which represent the passages through the original braincase wall (chipped away here of course) for the twelve cranial nerves. Other smaller pipes and tubes passing through the braincase wall are also preserved, and these hint at the distribution of a set of blood vessels that carried blood into the floor of the brain from the heart (via the carotid artery) and, of course, drained the blood away from the brain through the large lateral head veins that lead back down the neck.

Carnivores have a diet largely comprising meat. From a biochemical and nutritional perspective, a diet of meat is one of the simplest and most obvious of options for any creature. Most of the other creatures in the world are made of roughly similar chemicals as the carnivores that eat them. Their flesh is therefore a ready and rapidly assimilated source of food, provided the prey can be caught, sliced into chunks in the mouth using simple knife-like teeth (or even swallowed whole), and then quickly digested in the stomach.

This whole process has the potential to be relatively quick and biochemically very efficient in that little is likely to be wasted.

Herbivores face a rather more challenging problem. Plants are neither particularly nutritious nor readily assimilable when compared to animal flesh. Plants are primarily built from large quantities of cellulose, a material that gives them strength and rigidity. The crucial, and extremely awkward, point about this unique chemical, so far as animals are concerned, is that it is *completely indigestible*: there is simply nothing in the armoury of chemicals in our guts that can actually dissolve cellulose. As a result, the cellulose portion of plants passes straight through animals' guts as what we call roughage. So, how do herbivores survive on what appears to be such an unpromising diet?

Plant-eaters have successfully adapted to this diet because they exhibit a number of characteristic features. They have a good set of teeth with hard-wearing, durable, complex, and rough grinding surfaces, and powerful jaws and muscles that can be used to grind up plant tissues between the teeth to release the nutritionally usable 'cell sap' that is enclosed within plant cell walls. Herbivores eat large quantities of plant food in order to be able to extract sufficient nutrients from such comparatively nutrient-poor material. As a result, herbivores tend to have barrel-shaped bodies that accommodate large and complicated guts, which are necessary to store the large volumes of plants that they have to eat and allow sufficient time for digestion to take place. Herbivores' large guts house dense populations of microbes that live within special chambers or pouches in the gut wall; our appendix is a tiny vestige of such a chamber, and hints at herbivory in our primate ancestry. This symbiosis allows herbivorous animals to provide a warm, sheltered environment and constant supplies of food for the microbes; in their turn, the microbes have the ability to synthesize cellulase, an enzyme that digests cellulose and converts it into sugars that can then be absorbed by the host animal.

By most standards, *Iguanodon* (11 metres long and weighing about 3–4 tonnes) was a large herbivorous animal, and would have consumed plants in large quantities. Given this background information, questions about precisely how *Iguanodon* fed and assimilated its food can be explored in detail.

One persistent theory concerning its method of feeding was its suggested use of a long tongue to pull vegetation into the mouth. This began with Gideon Mantell, who described one of the first, nearly complete lower jaws of *Iguanodon*. The new fossil included some tell-tale teeth, so the ownership could not be doubted, and it had a toothless, spout-shaped front end. Mantell speculated that the spout shape allowed a long tongue to slide in and out of the mouth, rather like a giraffe's does. Mantell could not have known that the tip of the newly discovered lower jaw was incomplete and was capped by a predentary bone that filled in the 'spout'.

It is very curious to note that in the 1920s Louis Dollo provided further support for Mantell's conjecture. Dollo described a special opening in the predentary at the tip of the lower jaw; this formed a tunnel passing straight through the predentary bone that

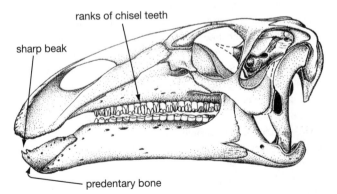

ranks of chisel teeth

sharp beak

predentary bone

26. *Iguanodon* skull

allowed a long, thin, muscular tongue to be projected outward to grasp vegetation and draw it into the mouth. Large bones (ceratobranchials) that had been found lying between the jaws of *Iguanodon* were suggested to act as the attachment for the muscles that would have operated this type of tongue. Such a structure fitted neatly with Dollo's concept of *Iguanodon* as a high arboreal browser with a giraffe-like long, grasping tongue.

Careful re-examination of the lower jaws of a number of *Iguanodon* skulls from Bernissart failed to reveal Dollo's predentary tunnel. The predentary has a sharp upper edge that supported a turtle-like horny beak. The predentary, and its beak, bit against the similarly toothless beak-covered premaxillae at the tip of the upper jaw, and this arrangement allowed these dinosaurs to very effectively crop the plants upon which they were feeding. The advantage of the horny beak was that it would have grown continuously (unlike teeth, which gradually wear away) no matter how tough and abrasive the plants that were being cropped. The ceratobranchial bones still require some explanation. In this instance, they would have been used to anchor the muscles that moved the tongue around the mouth to reposition the food as it was being chewed and for pushing the food back into the throat when it was ready to be swallowed. This is exactly the same role that is performed by the ceratobranchial bones in the floor of the human mouth.

How *Iguanodon* chewed its food

Apart from the horny beak that was able to nip off plants at the front end of the mouth, the sides of the jaws are lined with a formidable, nearly parallel array of chisel-like teeth that form irregularly edged blades (Figure 26). Each working tooth slots neatly against its neighbours in a rank-and-file arrangement, and beneath the working teeth are replacement crowns that will slot into place as the working teeth are worn away, forming what is in effect a 'magazine', or battery, of teeth. This continuous replacement pattern is normal for reptiles in general. What is unusual, even by reptile standards, is that the working and replacement teeth are held together in an ever-growing magazine as if they were all contributing to one giant, grindstone-like tooth. Wear between opposing (upper and lower) magazines maintains a grinding surface throughout the life of the dinosaur. Rather than having permanent, hard-wearing grinders (as we do), this could be described as a disposable model that relies on constant replacement of individually simpler teeth.

Opposing edges of each cutting blade of teeth have characteristics that ensure efficiency in their cutting action. The inner surfaces of the lower teeth are coated in a thick layer of extremely hard enamel, while the remainder of the tooth is made of softer, bone-like dentine. In contrast, the upper teeth have the reverse arrangement: the *outer* edge being coated in thick enamel and the remainder of the tooth is composed of dentine. When the jaws are closed, these opposing blades slide past each other: the hard, enamelled leading edge of the lower jaw magazine meets the enamelled cutting edge of the upper teeth in a cutting/shearing action rather like the blades of a pair of scissors (Figure 27). Once the enamelled edges have passed one another, the enamel edges (unlike scissor blades) then cut against the less resistant dentine parts of opposing magazines in a tearing and grinding action, which is ideal for crushing up tough plant fibres.

The geometry of the grinding surfaces of the upper and lower 'magazines' is particularly interesting. The worn surfaces are oblique, the lower surfaces face outward and upward, while the upper teeth have worn surfaces that face inward and downward. This pattern has interesting consequences. In conventional reptiles, the closure of the lower jaw is brought about by a simple hinge effect, with the jaws on either side of the mouth closing simultaneously in what is called an *isognathic* bite. If this type of bite is proposed for *Iguanodon*, then it is immediately obvious that the two sets of teeth on either side of the mouth would simply become permanently wedged together: the lower jaws jamming inside the upper ones. This means it is impossible to imagine how the angled wear surfaces could ever have developed in the first place.

For the angled wear surfaces to have developed, there would have had to be some ability of the jaws to move sideways as they closed. This type of movement is achieved in living herbivorous mammals through the development of an *anisognathic* jaw closure mechanism. This relies on the fact that the lower jaws are naturally narrower than the upper jaws. Special muscles, arranged in a sling on either side of each jaw bone, are capable to controlling the position of the jaw very precisely so that the teeth on one side meet one another and then the lower set is forcibly slid inwards so that the teeth grind against one another. We humans employ this type of jaw mechanism, especially when eating tough foods, but it is far more exaggerated in some classically herbivorous mammals such as cows, sheep, and goats, where the swing of the jaw is very obvious.

The whole mammalian type of jaw mechanism is dependent upon very complex jaw muscles, a complex nervous control system, and a specially constructed set of skull bones to withstand the stresses associated with this chewing method. By contrast, more conventional reptiles. of which *Iguanodon* was one, do not have an anisognathic jaw arrangement, lack the complex muscular arrangements that allow the lower jaw to be very precisely positioned (whether they had the nervous system to control such movements is largely irrelevant), and their skulls are not specially reinforced to withstand the lateral forces acting on the skull bones.

Iguanodon appears to present us with a conundrum: it does not fit any of the expected models. Is the anatomy wrong, or was this dinosaur doing something unexpected?

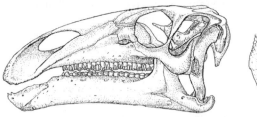

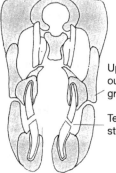

Upper jaw forced
outwards in
grinding motion

Teeth meet at
steep angle

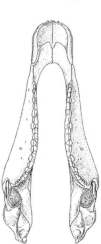

27. *Iguanodon* **teeth and jaws**

The lower jaws of *Iguanodon* are strong, and quite complex, bones.
At the front end each lower jaw is clamped to its neighbour by the
predentary bone. The teeth are arranged essentially parallel to
the length of the jaw, and at the rear there is a tall prong (coronoid
process) of bone which acts as an attachment area for powerful
jaw-closing muscles, and as a lever to improve the force of closure
that can be exerted on the teeth. Behind the coronoid process are a
group of tightly clustered bones that support the hinge-like jaw
joint. The upper jaws, during biting, would have been subjected not
only to vertical forces, created by the upward closure of the lower
jaws and teeth against the uppers, but also to sideways forces

generated by the lower teeth wedging themselves between the upper teeth as the bite force increased.

Of all forces acting on the skull of *Iguanodon*, the ones that it is least well-equipped to deal with are sideways forces acting on its teeth. The long snout (the area in front of the eye sockets) has a deep inverted 'U' shape in cross-section. To resist sideways forces acting on the teeth, the skull would need to be braced by bony 'joists' connecting the upper jaws; this is the arrangement found in living mammals. Without such bracing, the skull of *Iguanodon* is very vulnerable to splitting along its midline simply because the depth of the cheek bones creates great leverage against the roof of the snout from forces acting on the teeth. Midline breakage of the skull was avoided by the provision of hinges that are arranged diagonally down either side of the skull; these allow the sides of the skull to flex outward simultaneously as the lower teeth force their way between the upper ones. Other features deeper within the skull helped to provide control over the amount of movement that was possible along this hinge (so that the upper jaws did not simply flop around loosely).

This remarkable system I named *pleurokinesis* ('side movement'). On the one hand, the system can be seen as a means of avoiding catastrophic failure of the skull during normal biting. However, the pleurokinetic mechanism allows a *grinding* motion between opposing sets of teeth. This mimics the grinding motion achieved by herbivorous mammals in a totally different way.

This new chewing system could be linked to another important observation concerning dinosaurs such as *Iguanodon*. Its teeth are recessed (set inwards) from the side of the face. This creates a depression that might have been covered over by a fleshy cheek – another most un-reptilian feature. Given that the upper teeth slid past the lowers to cut up their food, it seems logical to expect that every time they bit through food in the mouth, at least half of it would be lost from the sides of the mouth . . . unless, of course, it was caught and recycled in the mouth by some sort of fleshy cheek. So these dinosaurs appeared to be not only capable of chewing their food in a surprisingly sophisticated way, but they also had mammal-like cheeks, and of course to aid the positioning of the food between the teeth before chews, they would have needed a big, muscular tongue (and strong ceratobranchials – the tongue-muscle bones).

Once this new chewing system had been identified, I was able to recognize that the pleurokinesis was not a 'one-off' invention associated with *Iguanodon*. It was actually widespread among the general group of dinosaurs known as ornithopods, to which *Iguanodon* belonged. Tracing the general evolutionary history of ornithopods across the Mesozoic Era, it became clear that these types of dinosaur became increasingly diverse and abundant in time. The ornithopods reached their greatest expression in the ecosystems of the latest Cretaceous period, at which time they are often reported as the most numerous of all land-animal fossils recovered. In some parts of the world, ornithopod dinosaurs, represented at this time by duck-billed or hadrosaurian dinosaurs, were exceedingly abundant and diverse: some discoveries in North America hint at herds of hadrosaurs numbering many tens of thousands of individuals. Hadrosaurs had the most sophisticated dental grinders (each of which had as many as 1,000 teeth in them at any one time) and a well-developed pleurokinetic system.

It seems plausible that these dinosaurs became abundant and diverse in large measure because they were very efficient at eating plant food, using the pleurokinetic system. Their evolutionary success was probably a result of their inheritance of the novel chewing mechanism first identified in *Iguanodon*.

Chapter 4
Unravelling the genealogy of dinosaurs

Up to this point, our focus has been largely, if not exclusively, tuned to exploring aspects of the anatomy, biology, and way of life of the dinosaur *Iguanodon*. It must be obvious that *Iguanodon* was just one dinosaur that fitted into far larger tableaux of life in the Mesozoic Era. One of the important tasks that falls to palaeontologists is to try to discover the genealogy, or evolutionary history, of the species that they study. To put dinosaurs as a whole into some sort of perspective, it will be necessary to outline the techniques used to do this, and our current understanding of dinosaurian evolutionary history.

One feature of the fossil record is that it offers the tantalizing possibility of tracing the genealogy of organisms not just over a few human generations (which is the ambit of modern genealogists) but over thousands, or millions, of generations, across the immensity of geological time. The primary means by which such research is carried out at present is the technique known as phylogenetic systematics. The premise of this technique is really quite simple. It accepts that organisms are subject to the general processes of Darwinian evolution. This does not require anything more profound than the assumption that organisms that are more closely related, in a genealogical sense, tend to physically resemble each other more closely than they do more distantly related creatures. To try to investigate the degree of relatedness of creatures (in this particular case fossil creatures), palaeosystematists are most interested in identifying as wide a range of anatomical features as are preserved in the hard parts of their fossils. Unfortunately, a great deal of really important biological information has simply rotted and been lost during the process of fossilization of any skeleton, so, being pragmatic about things, we simply have to make the most of what is left. Until quite recently, the reconstruction of phylogenies had relied on hard-part anatomical features of animals alone; however, technological innovations have now made it possible to compile data, based on the biochemical and molecular structure of living organisms, that can add significant and new information to the process.

What the dinosaur systematist has to do is compile lengthy lists of anatomical characteristics, with the intention of identifying those that are phylogenetically important, or contain an evolutionary signal. The task is intended to produce a workable hierarchy of relationship, based on groupings of ever more closely related animals.

The analysis also identifies features that are unique to a particular fossil species; these are important because they establish the special characteristics that, for example, distinguish *Iguanodon* from all other dinosaurs. This probably sounds blindingly obvious but, in truth, fossil creatures are often based on a small number of bones or teeth. If other partial remains are discovered in rocks elsewhere from the original, but of very similar age, it can be quite a challenge to prove convincingly whether the new remains belong to, say, *Iguanodon*, or perhaps a new and previously undiscovered creature.

Beyond the features that identify *Iguanodon* as unique, there is also a need to identify anatomical features that it shares with other equally distinct, but quite closely related animals. You might say that these were the equivalent of its anatomical 'family'. The more general the characters that 'family' groups of dinosaurs share, the

The case of *Baryonyx*

The Early Cretaceous rocks of south-east England have been intensely investigated by fossil hunters (starting with Gideon Mantell) and geologists (notably William Smith) for well over 200 years. *Iguanodon* bones are very common, as are the remains of a limited range of other dinosaurs, such as '*Megalosaurus*', *Hylaeosaurus*, *Polacanthus*, *Pelorosaurus*, *Valdosaurus*, and *Hypsilophodon*. Given the intensity of such work, it would be thought highly unlikely that anything new would ever be discovered. However, in 1983 the amateur collector William Walker discovered a large claw bone in a clay pit in Surrey that led to the excavation of an 8-metre-long predatory dinosaur that was entirely new to science. It was named *Baryonyx walkeri* in honour of its discoverer, and has pride of place on exhibition at the Natural History Museum in London.

The moral of this story is that nothing should be taken for granted; the fossil record is likely to be full of surprises.

more this allows them to be grouped into ever larger and more inclusive categories of dinosaurs that gradually piece together an overall pattern of relationships for them all.

The real question is: how is this overall pattern of relationships achieved? For a very long time, the general method that was used might be described simply as 'I know best'. It was quite literally the view of self-styled experts, who had spent much time studying a particular group of organisms and then summarized the overall patterns of similarity for their group; their methods for doing this might vary considerably, but in the end their preferred pattern of relationship was little more than just that: their preference, rather than a rigorous, scientifically debated solution. While this method worked reasonably well for restricted groups of organisms, it proved far more difficult to properly debate the validity of one interpretation compared with another because the arguments, when boiled down to their essentials, were circular, relying on one person's belief over another's.

This underlying problem was brought into sharp focus when groups of organisms were very large in number and varied in many subtle ways. Good examples are groups of insects, or some of the bewildering varieties of bony fish. If the general scientific community was happy to accept the authority of one scientist for a period of time then all was apparently fine. However, if experts could not agree, the end result was frustratingly circular debates.

Over the past four decades, a new methodology has gradually been adopted that has proved far more valuable scientifically. It does not necessarily give the correct answers, but it is at least open to scientific scrutiny and real debate. This technique is now widely known as cladistics (phylogenetic systematics). The name is treated with a fair degree of trepidation by some, but this is largely because there have been some very fierce arguments about how cladistics is done in practice and what the overall significance of the results might be in an evolutionary context. Fortunately, we do not need to consider much of this debate because the principles are actually surprisingly simple and clear-cut.

A cladogram is a branching tree diagram that links together all the species that are being investigated at the time. To create one, the researcher needs to compile a table (data matrix) containing a column listing the species under consideration and against this a compilation of the features (anatomical, biochemical, etc.) that each species exhibits. Each species is then 'scored' in relation to whether it does (1) or does not (0) possess each character, or in some instances if the decision is uncertain this can be signified as a (?). The resulting matrix of data (these can be very large) is then analysed using a number of proprietary computer programs, whose role is to assess the distribution of 1s and 0s and generate a set of statistics that determines the most parsimonious distribution of the data that are shared by the various species. The resulting cladogram forms the starting point for a considerable amount of further investigation that is aimed at determining and understanding the degree to which there are common patterns or overall similarities, and the extent to which the data might be misleading or erroneous.

The cladogram that results from this type of analysis represents no more than a working hypothesis of the relationships of the animals that are being investigated. Each of the branches on the tree mark points at which it is possible to define a group of species that are all connected by their sharing a number of characteristic features. And using this information it is possible to construct what is, in effect, a sort of genealogy or phylogeny representing a model of the evolutionary history of the group as a whole. For example, if the known geological times of occurrence of each of the species are plotted on to this pattern, it becomes possible to indicate the overall history of the group, and also the probable time at which various of the species may have originated. In this way, the cladogram, rather than simply representing a convenient spatial arrangement of species, begins to resemble a real genealogy. Obviously, each such phylogeny created in this way is only as good as the data available, and the data and how it is scored can change with the discovery of new, better, or more complete fossils, and also as new methods of analysis are developed or older ones are improved upon.

The aim of all this work is to help create as accurate a picture as possible of the evolutionary history of life or, in this particular case, the evolutionary history of dinosaurs.

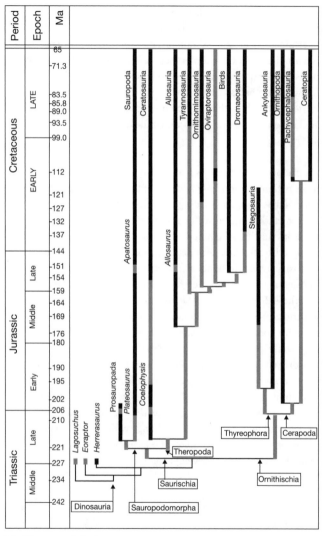

28. Dinosaur cladogram

An evolutionary history of the dinosaurs: in brief

An interesting example of this type of systematic approach to the evolution of dinosaurs is represented by the work of Paul Sereno of the University of Chicago. Sereno has spent considerable time, over the past two decades, investigating the systematics and general evolutionary history of dinosaurs. Figure 28 summarizes this work and permits an all too brief overview.

Dinosauria are traditionally recognized (as Owen so perceptively saw) as reptiles with an upright leg posture and specially reinforced connections between the hips and vertebral column to facilitate the efficient carriage of the body on its pillar-like legs. These changes conferred upon early dinosaurs some highly valuable assets: pillar-like legs could support great body weight very effectively and dinosaurs could become very large creatures; and, pillar-like legs allow a long stride, meaning that some dinosaurs could move very quickly. Both attributes were used very effectively by dinosaurs throughout their reign on Earth.

While all dinosaurs share these crucial features, they can be divided into two fundamentally different types: the Saurischia (literally, 'lizard-hipped') and Ornithischia ('bird-hipped'). As these names suggest, the differences between such dinosaurs lie primarily in the structure of their hip bones, although several other more subtle anatomical features are important in helping to distinguish these two major types. The earliest members of both groups of dinosaur have been identified in rocks of Carnian age (at least 225 Ma), but it has not been possible to identify the earliest dinosaur of all or whether it was strictly a saurischian, ornithischian, or just a dinosaurian that was not yet either.

Saurischian dinosaurs

Saurischians include two major groups. Sauropodomorpha are mainly large-bodied creatures with pillar-like legs, extraordinarily long tails, long necks ending in small heads, and jaws lined with simple, peg-shaped teeth, indicating a mainly herbivorous diet. These include such giants as members of the diplodocoid, brachiosauroid (Figure 31), and titanosaurian groups. Theropoda are markedly different to their sauropodomorph relatives. They are almost entirely agile, bipedal, and predominantly meat-eating dinosaurs (Figures 30, 31). A long, muscular tail counterbalances the front of the body at the hip, leaving the arms and hands free to be used to grab their prey; their heads also tend to be rather large, and their jaws lined with sharp, knife-like teeth. These types of dinosaur range from small and rather delicate creatures similar to *Compsognathus*, which are commonly referred to as coelurosaurs, through to such enormous creatures such as the legendary *Tyrannosaurus*, while other equally large and fearsome-looking theropods include *Giganotosaurus*, *Allosaurus*, *Baryonyx*, and *Spinosaurus*. Although some of these dinosaurs may be well known, the group as a whole is proving to be extraordinarily diverse, and in some cases quite bizarre. Newly discovered therizinosaurs, for example, appear to have been huge, lumbering creatures with long, scythe-like claws on their hands, enormous bellies, and ridiculously small heads whose jaws were lined with teeth that are far more reminiscent of plant-eaters than conventional meat-eaters. Yet other theropods known as ornithomimians and oviraptorians were lightly built, rather ostrich-like creatures that were entirely toothless (and therefore beaked just like living birds). However, the source of greatest interest among this entire group of dinosaurs is the subgroup known as dromaeosaurians.

Dromaeosaurians include such renowned creatures as *Velociraptor* and *Deinonychus*, and a host of similar but less famous creatures that have been discovered recently. Their particular interest lies in the fact that their skeletal anatomy is closely similar to that of living birds; indeed, the similarities are so great that they are thought to be direct bird ancestors. Dramatic new discoveries, at sites in Liaoning Province, China, that exhibit truly exceptional preservational conditions, of dromaeosaurian theropods reveal a

29. *Deinonychus.* **A reconstruction from bone to flesh. Perhaps it too had a filamentous covering?**

body covering made of either keratinous filaments (like a coarse form of hair) or in some cases genuinely bird-like feathers, which emphasizes their similarity to modern birds.

Ornithischian dinosaurs

All ornithischians are thought to have been herbivorous and, rather like modern-day mammals, they seem to be far more diverse, and numerous, than their potential predators.

Thyreophorans (Figure 28) are a major group of ornithischians that

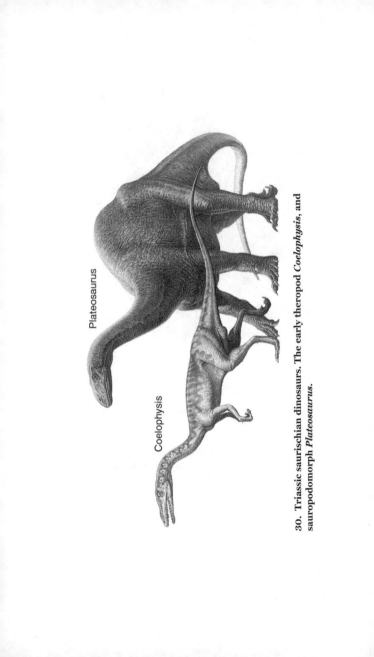

Plateosaurus

Coelophysis

30. Triassic saurischian dinosaurs. The early theropod *Coelophysis*, and sauropodomorph *Plateosaurus*.

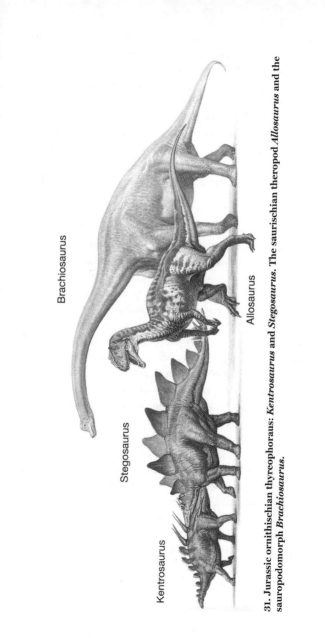

Brachiosaurus

Stegosaurus

Allosaurus

Kentrosaurus

31. Jurassic ornithischian thyreophoraus: *Kentrosaurus* and *Stegosaurus*. The saurischian theropod *Allosaurus* and the sauropodomorph *Brachiosaurus*.

are characterized by bearing bony plates in their body wall, clubs or spikes adorning their tails, and for having an almost exclusively quadrupedal method of locomotion. These types of dinosaur include the stegosaurs, named after the iconic *Stegosaurus* (well known for its tiny head, the rows of large bony plates on its back, and its spiky tail (Figure 31)); and the heavily armoured ankylosaurs including such creatures as *Euoplocephalus*. The latter was a huge tank-like animal that was so heavily armour-plated that even its eyelids were reinforced by bony shutters and its tail was terminated in a huge, bony club that it presumably used to skittle potential predators.

Cerapodans (Figure 28) were very different to thyreophorans. These were typically lightly built, unarmoured bipeds, although a few did revert to quadrupedal methods of locomotion. Ornithopods were one major group of cerapodans. Many of these dinosaurs were medium-sized (2–5 metres long) and quite abundant (probably filling the ecological niches occupied by antelopes, deer, sheep, and goats today). These animals, such as *Hypsilophodon*, were balanced at the hip (just like theropods), had slender legs for fast running, grasping hands, and, most importantly, teeth, jaws, and cheeks adapted for a diet of plants. Throughout the reign of the dinosaurs, small to medium-sized ornithopods were quite abundant, but through the Mesozoic a significant number of larger types evolved; these are known as iguanodontians (because they include animals such as *Iguanodon*). Most important of all the iguanodontians were the extraordinarily numerous duck-billed, or hadrosaurian, dinosaurs of the Late Cretaceous of North America and Asia. Some (but not all) of these dinosaurs did indeed have rather duck-shaped snouts, and others had a wide range of quite extravagant, hollow-crested headgear (see Chapter 7); this headgear may well have been used for social signalling, and more particularly for making loud, honking sounds. Marginocephalians were the other major cerapodan group and appeared in Cretaceous times. These included the extraordinary pachycephalosaurs ('thick-headed dinosaurs'); they had bodies that were very similar in general appearance to the ornithopods, but their heads were very odd-looking. The majority had a high dome of bone on the top, which looked vaguely similar to the headgear of hadrosaurians, except for the fact that pachycephalosaur headgear was made of solid bone. It has been suggested that these creatures were the 'headbangers' of the Cretaceous world – perhaps using head clashing in similar fashion to that seen among some cloven-hooved animals today.

Finally, there were the ceratopians, a group of dinosaurs that included the fabled *Protoceratops* referred to in the Introduction, as well as the well-known *Triceratops* ('three-horned face'). All had a singular narrow beak at the tip of the jaws and tended to have a ruff-like collar of bone at the back edge of the skull. While some of these dinosaurs, particularly the early ones, maintained a bipedal way of life, a considerable number grew greatly in body size, with an enlarged head, which was adorned with a huge frill-like collar and large eyebrow and nose horns. Their great bulk and heavy head led them to adopt a four-footed stance, and their similarity to modern-day rhinoceros has not gone unnoticed. Clearly, as this all too brief survey shows, dinosaurs were many and varied, judging by the discoveries made over the past 200 years. But even though to date about 900 genera of dinosaurs are known, this is only a tiny fraction of the dinosaurs that lived during the 160 million years of their reign during the Mesozoic Era. Many of these will, unfortunately, never be known: their fossils were never preserved. Others will be discovered by intrepid dinosaur hunters in years to come.

Dinosaur systematics and ancient biogeography

This type of research can have interesting, if slightly unexpected, spin-offs. One spin-off that will be considered here links phylogenetics with the geographic history of the Earth. The Earth may in fact have exerted a profound influence on the overall pattern of life.

The geological timescale of the Earth was pieced together through painstaking analysis of the relative ages of sequences of rocks exposed at various places on Earth. One important component that assisted this process was the evidence of the fossils that they contained: if rocks from different places contained fossils of exactly the same type, then it could be assumed with reasonable confidence that the rocks were of the same relative age.

In broadly similar fashion, evidence of the similarity of fossils from different parts of the world began to suggest that the continents might not have been as fixed in their positions as they appear to be today. For example, it had been noted that rocks and the fossils that they contained seemed to be remarkably similar on either side of the southern Atlantic Ocean. A small aquatic reptile *Mesosaurus* was known to exist in remarkably similar-looking Permian rocks in Brazil and in South Africa. As long ago as 1620, Francis Bacon had pointed out that the coastlines of the Americas and Europe and Africa seemed remarkably similar, (see Figure 32d) to the extent that it seemed as if they could have fitted together as a pair of gigantic jigsaw pieces. On the basis of evidence from fossils, rocks, and general shape correspondence, Alfred Wegener, a German meteorologist, suggested in 1912 that at times in the past the continents of the Earth must have occupied different positions to the ones they are in today, with, for example, the Americas and Eur-Africa nestled together in the Permian Period. Because he was not a trained geologist, Wegener's views were ignored, or dismissed as irrelevant and unprovable speculations. For all its self-evident persuasiveness, Wegener's theory lacked a mechanism: common sense dictated that it was impossible to move things the size of continents across the solid surface of the Earth.

However, common sense proved to be deceptive. In the 1950s and 1960s, a series of observations accumulated that supported Wegener's views. Firstly, very detailed models of all the major continents showed that they did indeed fit together remarkably neatly and with a correspondence that could not be accounted for by chance. Secondly, major geological features on separate continents became continuous when continents were reassembled jigsaw-like. And finally, palaeomagnetic evidence demonstrated the phenomenon of sea-floor spreading – that the ocean floors were moving like huge conveyor belts carrying the continents – and the historical remnants of magnetism in continental rocks confirmed that the continents had moved over time. The 'motor' that was driving this motion was in effect the heat at the core and the fluidity of rocks in the mantle layer inside the Earth. The theory of plate tectonics that accounts for the movement of continents over the surface of the Earth over time is now well established and corroborated.

From a dinosaur evolutionary perspective, the implications of plate tectonics are extremely interesting. Reconstructions of past configurations of the continents, largely based on palaeomagnetics and detailed stratigraphy, indicate that at the time of their origin all the continents were lying clustered together in a single gigantic landmass, known as Pangaea ('all Earth') (Figure 32a). Dinosaurs at this time were quite literally capable of walking all over the Earth, and in reflection of this it appears to be the case that the fossil remains of rather similar types (theropods and prosauropods) have been found on nearly all continents.

During subsequent Periods, the Jurassic (Figure 32b) and Cretaceous (Figure 32c), it is evident that the supercontinent began to fragment as the immensely powerful tectonic conveyor belts imperceptibly, but remorselessly, wrenched Pangaea apart. The end product of this process at the close of the Cretaceous was a world that, though still different geographically (note particularly the position of India in Figure 32c), has some very familiar-looking continents.

The earliest dinosaurs seem to have been able to disperse across much of Pangaea, judging by their fossils. However, during the Jurassic and subsequent Cretaceous Periods it was clearly the case

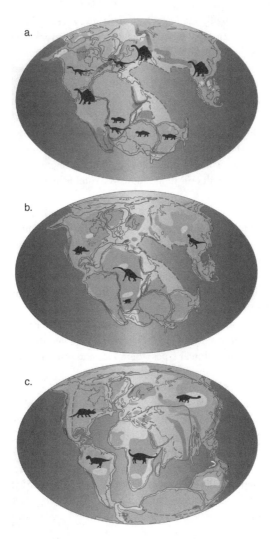

32. The changing continents. a. Triassic Period showing the single supercontinent called Pangaea. b. Middle Jurassic Period. c. Early Cretaceous Period. Note that the dinosaur images become increasingly different as the continents separate from one another.

d.

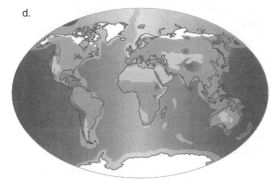

32(d). The continents as they are today. Close the Atlantic Ocean and the Americas fit neatly against West Africa.

that the unified supercontinent became gradually subdivided by intervening seaways as continent-sized fragments gradually drifted apart.

An inevitable biological consequence of this intrinsic (Earth-bound) process of continental sundering is that the once cosmopolitan population of dinosaurs became progressively subdivided and isolated. The phenomenon of isolation is one of the keystones of organismal evolution – once isolated, populations of organisms tend to undergo evolutionary change in response to local changes to their immediate environment. In this instance, although we are dealing with comparatively huge (continent-sized) areas, each of the continental fragments carried its own population of dinosaurs (and associated fauna and flora); each of which, with the passing time, had the opportunity to evolve independently in response to local changes in environment, stimulated by, for example, progressive changes in latitude, longitude, adjacent oceanic currents, and prevailing atmospheric conditions.

Logic dictates that it must clearly have been the case that tectonic events during the Mesozoic affected the scope and overall pattern of the evolutionary history of dinosaurs. Indeed, it seems perfectly reasonable to suppose that the progressive fragmentation of ancestral populations over time must have done much to accelerate the diversification of the group as a whole. Just as we can represent the phylogeny of dinosaurs using cladograms, we could also represent the geographic history of the Earth through the Mesozoic Era as a series of branching events as continental areas separated from the 'ancestral' Pangaean Earth. Of course, this general approach is a simplification of true Earth history because, on occasion, continental fragments have coalesced, welding together previously isolated populations. But at least as a first approximation, this provides a fertile area for investigating some of the larger-scale events in Earth history.

If this model of the natural history of dinosaurs were generally true, we might expect to be able to detect some evidence in its support by probing the details of the fossil record of dinosaur species, and the tectonic models of continental distribution through the Mesozoic. This type of approach has been developed in recent years to probe for coincident patterns in the evolutionary history of dinosaurs and whether their evolutionary history is echoed in their geographic distribution.

Ornithopod evolution

The earliest work in this field of research, carried out in 1984, concerned a group of dinosaurs that are quite closely related to the familiar *Iguanodon*. Generally, these types of dinosaur are known as ornithopods ('bird feet' – this comes from a passing, trivial resemblance in the structure of the feet of these dinosaurs to those of modern birds). Comparing in some detail the anatomy of a number of the then known ornithopods, a cladogram was constructed. To convert this into a genuine phylogeny it was necessary to chart on to the cladogam the known distribution of this group through time and their geographic distributions.

Some surprising patterns in the history of these ornithopod dinosaurs emerged from this analysis. First it seemed to demonstrate that the forms most closely related to *Iguanodon* (that is to say, members of the group known as iguanodonts) and their closest relatives (members of the hadrosaur family) probably originated as a result of continental separation during Late Jurassic times. The ancestral population from which both groups may have evolved became subdivided by a seaway at this time. Following this isolation, one population evolved into the hadrosaurs in Asia, while iguanodonts evolved elsewhere. These two groups appear to have evolved distinct from one another through the Late Jurassic and Early Cretaceous period. However, during the latter half of the Cretaceous, Asia became reconnected to the rest of the northern hemisphere continents and its hadrosaurs were apparently able to spread across the northern hemisphere pretty much unhindered and replaced iguanodonts wherever they came into contact.

While the pattern of replacement of iguanodonts by hadrosaurs in Late Cretaceous times appeared to be reasonably uniform, there were one or two puzzling anomalies that needed to be investigated.

There were reports, written at the turn of the 20th century, of iguanodonts from Europe (primarily France and Romania) in rocks of very latest Cretaceous age. From the analysis above, these would not have been expected to have survived into Late Cretaceous times because everywhere else the pattern was one of hadrosaurs replacing iguanodonts. In the early 1990s, the best-preserved material came from Transylvania, a region of Romania. However, the phylogenetic analysis prompted expeditions to reinvestigate these discoveries. Fresh study proved that this dinosaur was not a close relative of *Iguanodon*, but represented an unusually long-lasting (relict) member of a more primitive group of ornithopods. An entirely new name was created for this dinosaur: *Zalmoxes*. So, one of the outcomes of the preliminary analysis was a great deal of new information about an old, but apparently not so well understood, dinosaur.

A report published in the 1950s suggested that a very *Iguanodon*-like dinosaur lived in Mongolia in Early Cretaceous times. This tantalizing report also needed to be investigated further to check whether its anomalous geographic range – in Asia in Early Cretaceous times – was real or, as in the Romanian example, another case of mistaken identity. The material, though fragmentary, was stored in the Russian Palaeontological Museum in Moscow, and had to be re-examined. What emerged was again not as expected. This time the earlier reports proved correct, the genus *Iguanodon* itself seemed to be present in Mongolia in Early Cretaceous times, and the pieces recovered were indistinguishable from the very well known European *Iguanodon*.

This second discovery did not fit at all comfortably with the evolutionary and geographic hypothesis that had been created in the 1984 analysis. Indeed, in more recent years a suite of very interesting *Iguanodon*-like ornithopods have emerged in Asia, as well as North America, in what can best be described as 'middle' Cretaceous times. Much of this very recent, and steadily accumulating, evidence suggests that the original evolutionary and geographic model had a number of fundamental flaws that continued investigation and new discoveries were able to expose.

Dinosaurs: a global perspective

In more recent times, this approach has been applied much more broadly and in a much more ambitious way. Paul Upchurch of University College London and Craig Hunn at Cambridge hoped to explore the entire family tree of the Dinosauria for evidence of similarities in patterns of stratigraphic ranges and cladistic patterns by looking at large numbers of dinosaurs. These were compared to the currently established distributions of the continents at intervals through the entire Mesozoic Era. An attempt was being made to find out whether an overall signal did emerge that was suggestive of a tectonic influence on the evolutionary history of all dinosaurs.

Despite the inevitable 'noise' in the system resulting largely from the incompleteness of the fossil record of dinosaurs, it was heartening to note that statistically significant coincident patterns emerged within the Middle Jurassic, the Late Jurassic, and the Early Cretaceous intervals. This indicates that tectonic events do, as expected, play some role in determining where and when particular groups of dinosaurs flourished. What is more, this effect has also been preserved in the stratigraphic and geographic distributions of other fossil organisms, so the evolutionary history of great swathes of organisms was effected by tectonic events and the imprint is still with us today. In a way, this is not new. I need only point to the unusual distribution of marsupial mammals (found only in the Americas and Australasia today), and the fact that distinct areas of the modern world have their own characteristic fauna and flora. What this new research suggests is that we may well be able to trace the historical reasons for these distributions far more accurately than we had supposed possible.

Chapter 5
Dinosaurs and warm blood

A number of areas of research on dinosaurs have attracted attention far beyond the realm of those who take a purely academic interest in these creatures. This common interest appears to arise because dinosaurs capture the public imagination in a way that few other subjects do. The following chapters focus on these topics in order to illustrate the extraordinary variety of approaches and types of information that are used in our attempts to unravel the mystery of dinosaurs and their biology.

Dinosaurs: hot-, cold-, or luke-warm-blooded?

As we have seen in Chapter 1, Richard Owen, at the time of his invention of the word 'dinosaur', speculated about the physiology of dinosaurs. Extracting meaning from the rather long-winded final sentence of his scientific report:

> The Dinosaurs ... may be concluded to have ... [a] superior adaptation to terrestrial life ... approaching that which now characterizes the warm-blooded Vertebrata. [i.e. living mammals and birds]

> (Owen 1842: 204)

Although the 'mammaloid' reconstructions of dinosaurs that he created for the Crystal Palace Park clearly echo his sentiments, the biological implications he was hinting at were never grasped by other workers at the time. In a sense, Owen's visionary approach was tempered by rational Aristotelian logic: dinosaurs were structurally reptilian, it therefore followed that they had scaly skins, laid shelled eggs, and, like all other known reptiles, were 'cold-blooded' (ectothermic).

In a similar vein to Owen, Thomas Huxley proposed, almost 50 years later, that birds and dinosaurs should be considered close relatives because of the anatomical similarities that could be demonstrated between living birds, the earliest known fossil bird *Archaeopteryx*, and the newly discovered small theropod *Compsognathus*. He concluded that:

> ... it is by no means difficult to imagine a creature completely intermediate between *Dromaeus* [an emu] and *Compsognathus* [a dinosaur] ... and the hypothesis that the ... class *Aves* has its root in the Dinosaurian reptiles; ...

> (Huxley 1868: 365)

If Huxley was correct, it should have been possible to ask: were dinosaurs then conventionally reptilian (physiologically) or were they closer to the 'warm-blooded' (endothermic) birds? There appeared to be no obvious way of answering such questions.

Despite such intellectual 'nudges', it was close to a century after Huxley's paper that palaeontologists began to search with greater determination for data that might have a bearing on this central question. The spur to renewed interest in the topic finds an echo in the adoption of the broader and more integrated agenda for the interpretation of the fossil record: the rise of *palaeobiology*, as outlined in Chapter 2. We saw there how some wide-ranging observations were strung together by Robert Bakker into a case for endothermy in dinosaurs. Let's now consider these and other arguments in greater detail.

New approaches: dinosaurs as climatic proxies?

Attempts were being made to investigate the degree to which fossils could be used to reconstruct climates in the ancient world. It is widely recognized that endotherms (basically mammals and birds) are not particularly good indicators of climate because they are found everywhere, from equatorial to polar regions. Their endothermic physiology (and clever use of body insulation) allows them to operate more or less independently of prevailing climatic conditions. By contrast, ectotherms, such as lizards, snakes, and crocodiles, are reliant on ambient climatic conditions, and as a result they tend to be found mainly in warmer climatic zones.

Using this approach to examine the geographic distribution of obvious ectotherms and endotherms in the fossil record proved useful, but then threw up several interesting questions. For example, what about the immediate evolutionary ancestors of endothermic mammals in Permian and Triassic times? Were they also able to control their internal body temperatures? If they did, how would it have affected their geographic distribution? And more pointedly in this context, dinosaurs seemed to have a wide geographic spread, so did this mean that they were capable of controlling their body temperature rather like endotherms?

Patterns in the fossil record

The foundation of Bakker's approach to endothermy in dinosaurs was the pattern in the succession of animal types in the early Mesozoic. During the time leading up to the end of the Triassic Period synapsid reptiles were by far the most abundant and diverse animals on land.

Right at the close of the Triassic and the beginning of the Jurassic Period (205 Ma) the very first true mammals appeared on Earth and were represented by small, shrew-like creatures. In complete contrast, the latter part of the Triassic Period also marks the appearance of the first dinosaurs (225 Ma), and across the Triassic/Jurassic divide the dinosaurs become widespread, very diverse, and clearly dominant members of the land fauna. This ecological balance – rare, small, very probably nocturnal mammals and abundant, large, and increasingly diverse dinosaurs – was then maintained for the next 160 million years, until the close of the Cretaceous Period (65 Ma).

As animals living in the present day, we are comfortable with the notion that mammals are, along with birds, the most conspicuous and diverse of land-living vertebrates. Mammals are self-evidently fast-moving, intelligent, generally highly adaptable creatures, and much of this present-day 'success' we attribute to their physiological status: their high basal metabolic rate, which permits the maintenance of a high and constant body temperature, complex body chemistry, comparatively large brains, and consequently high activity levels, and their status as endotherms. In contrast, we generally observe that reptiles are considerably less diverse and quite sharply climatically restricted; this is largely explained by the fact that they have a much lower metabolic rate, rely on external sources of heat to keep the body warm and therefore chemically active, and have much lower and more intermittent levels of activity: the ectothermic condition.

These, admittedly very general, observations permit us to have expectations that can be superimposed on the fossil record. All things being equal, we would predict that the first appearance of true mammals at the Triassic/Jurassic boundary, in a world otherwise dominated by reptiles, would spark the former's rapid evolutionary rise and diversification at the expense of the latter. So the fossil record of mammals would be expected to show a rapid rise in abundance and diversity in Early Jurassic times, until they completely dominated the ecosystems of the Mesozoic Era. However, the fossil record reveals exactly the opposite pattern: the (reptilian) dinosaurs rose to dominance in the Late Triassic (220 Ma) and the mammals only began to increase in size and diversity after the dinosaurs had become extinct at the end of the Cretaceous period (65 Ma).

Bakker's explanation for this counterintuitive set of events was that dinosaurs could have succeeded, evolutionarily, in the face of true mammals only if they too had endotherm-like high basal metabolic rates and could be as active and resourceful as contemporary mammals. Dinosaurs quite simply *had* to be active endotherms – it was to Bakker a self-evident truth. While the pattern revealed by the fossil record was indeed clear, the scientific proof necessary to support his 'truth' needed to be assembled and tested.

Legs, heads, hearts, and lungs

Dinosaurs place their feet vertically beneath the body on straight, pillar-like legs. The only living creatures that also adopt this posture are birds and mammals; all the rest 'sprawl' with their legs directed sideways from the body. Many dinosaurs were also slender-limbed and apparently built for moving quickly; this line of argument reflects the fact that Nature does not tend to do things unnecessarily. If an animal is built as if it could run fast, it probably did so; it might therefore seem reasonable to expect such a creature to have an energetic 'motor', or endothermic physiology, to allow it to move quickly. We do, however, need to be careful, because it is also the case that ectotherms can move very quickly indeed – crocodiles and Komodo dragons can outrun and catch unwary humans! The crucial thing is that crocodiles and Komodo dragons cannot sustain fast running – their muscles build up a large oxygen debt very quickly and the animals then have to rest so their muscles can recover. Endotherms, by contrast, can move quickly for much longer periods of time because their high-pressure blood system and efficient lungs replenish the oxygen in their muscles very quickly.

A further refinement of this argument is the suggestion that the ability to walk bipedally is linked exclusively to endothermy; many mammals, all birds, and many dinosaurs are bipedal. This argument relates not only to posture, but also to how that posture is maintained. A quadruped has the advantage of considerable stability when it walks. A biped is inherently unstable, and to walk successfully a sophisticated system of sensors monitoring balance, as well as a rapid coordinating system (the brain and central nervous system), and rapid-response muscles to correct and maintain balance, are essential.

The brain is central to this whole dynamic 'problem' and must have a constant capacity to work quickly and efficiently. This implies that the body is able to provide constant supplies of oxygen, food, and heat to allow the chemistry of the brain to work optimally all the time. The prerequisite for this type of stability is a 'steady' endothermic physiology. Ectotherms periodically shut down their activity levels, when cold, for example, and reduce the supply of nutrients to the brain, which is consequentially less sophisticated and closely integrated to overall body functions.

Another posture-related observation can be linked to the efficiency of the heart and its potential to sustain high activity levels. Many birds, mammals, and dinosaurs adopt an upright body posture in which the head is normally held at levels appreciably higher than the position of the heart. This difference in head-heart level has important hydrostatic consequences. Because the head is above the heart, it has to be capable of pumping blood at high pressure 'up' to the brain. But the blood that is pumped at the same time with each heartbeat from the heart to the lungs must circulate at low pressure, otherwise it would burst the delicate capillaries that line the lungs. To permit this pressure difference, the heart in mammals and birds is physically divided down the middle, so that the left side of the heart (the systemic, or head and body, circuit) can run at a higher pressure than the right side (the pulmonary, or lung, circuit).

All living reptiles carry their head at roughly the same level as their heart. Their hearts are not divided down the middle like those of mammals and birds because there is no need to differentiate between the systemic and pulmonary circuits. Curiously, the reptilian heart and circulation offers advantages for these creatures; they can shunt blood around the body in ways that mammals cannot. For example, ectotherms spend a lot of time basking in the sun to warm their bodies. While basking, they can preferentially shunt blood to the skin, where it can be used to absorb heat (rather like the water in solar panel central heating pipes). The major disadvantage of this system is that the blood cannot be circulated under high pressure – a feature that is essential in any animal that is behaving very actively and must bring food and oxygen to its hard-working muscles.

The implication from all these considerations is that dinosaurs, because of their posture, had a high-pressure blood circulation system that was compatible with high and sustained activity levels that are only found in living endotherms. This more comprehensive and elaborate set of considerations resoundingly supports Richard Owen's provocative speculation.

Intimately associated with the efficiency of the heart and circulatory system must be the ability to supply sufficient oxygen to muscles to allow high levels of aerobic activity. In some groups of dinosaurs, notably the theropods and the giant sauropodomorphs, there are some tantalizing anatomical hints concerning lung structure and function. In both these groups of saurischian dinosaurs (but not the ornithischians), there are traces of distinct pouches or cavities (called pleurocoels) in the sides of the vertebrae of the backbone. In isolation, these might not have attracted particular attention; however, living birds show similar features that equate with the presence of extensive air sacs. Air sacs are part of a bellows-like mechanism that permits birds to breathe with remarkable efficiency. It is highly probable that saurischian dinosaurs had bird-like, and therefore extremely efficient, lungs.

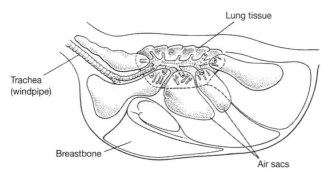

Lung tissue

Trachea (windpipe)

Breastbone

Air sacs

33. Bird air sacs provide for a highly efficient respiratory system

This observation certainly supports the contention that some dinosaurs (theropods and sauropodomorphs) had the ability to maintain high aerobic activity levels. However, it also highlights the fact that all dinosaurs (saurischians *and* ornithischians) should not be presumed to have been the same in all aspects of their physiology, because ornithischians show no trace of an air-sac system.

Dinosaur 'sophistication' and brain size

Although the line of argument that follows is not universal to dinosaurs, it is instructive in the sense that it shows what *some* dinosaurs were capable of doing. The classic example is John Ostrom's dromaeosaur *Deinonychus* (Figure 29). As was summarized in Chapter 2, this dinosaur was a large-eyed visual predator that could clearly run fast, judging by its limb proportions and general build. In addition, it had an unusual stiff, narrow tail, extraordinary gaff-like inner toes on its hind feet, and long, sharply clawed, grasping arms. It is not unreasonable to suggest that this animal was built as a pursuit predator, was capable of using its narrow tail as a dynamic balancing aid (flicking the tail to one side or the other would allow this animal to change direction extremely quickly), and very probably leapt at its prey, which it then disabled using the claws on its feet. We have never seen a *Deinonychus* in action, but this scenario is based upon observable features of the skeleton, and is partially supported by one remarkable fossil discovered in Mongolia.

The latter comprises two dinosaurs, the small herbivorous ceratopian *Protoceratops* and a close relative of *Deinonychus* known as *Velociraptor*. This extraordinary fossil shows the two creatures caught in a death struggle; they probably choked to death in a dust storm while fighting with each other. The *Velociraptor* is preserved clinging to the head of its prey using its long arms, and in the very act of kicking at the throat of its unfortunate victim.

Such overall 'sophistication' in design, inferred function, and way of life strongly suggests activity levels that are more similar to those exhibited by modern endotherms.

Echoing some of the argument seen in the discussion concerning dinosaurs' ability to move bipedally, the brains of both mammals and birds are large and both groups exhibit what appears to be intelligent behaviour. In contrast, ectothermic reptiles possess smaller brains and are not usually renowned for their intellectual prowess (though this is in part a fiction that we have propagated). There does, however, appear to be a general link between overall brain size and endothermy. Large brains are highly complex structures that demand constant supplies of oxygen and food, as well as a stable temperature in order to function efficiently. Ectothermic reptiles clearly can supply both food and oxygen to their brains effectively, but their body temperature does vary across a normal 24-hour cycle, and as a consequence they are unable to supply the needs of a large and sophisticated brain.

Tradition has it that dinosaurs were notoriously lacking in brain power (the walnut-sized *Stegosaurus* brain is often cited as a classic example). However, Jim Hopson at the University of Chicago has done much to rectify this somewhat erroneous view. Comparing the ratio of brain volume to body volume across a range of animals, including dinosaurs, Hopson was able to demonstrate that most dinosaurs had fairly typically reptile-sized brains. Some, however, were unexpectedly well endowed in the 'brains department' – not surprisingly perhaps, these were the highly active, bipedal theropods.

Latitudinal distributions

Earlier in this chapter it was mentioned that charting distributional data had been one of the spurs to pursuing the physiological status of dinosaurs. Recently, reports have shown numbers of dinosaurs in the Yukon area of North America as well as in Australia and Antarctica. These areas would have fallen within their respective polar regions in Cretaceous times, and have been used to support the idea that dinosaurs must have been endothermic to have survived. It is, after all, clearly the case today that ectothermic land vertebrates are incapable of living at such high latitudes.

However, upon careful consideration, these observations are not as persuasive as they seem at first sight. Evidence from the plant fossil record suggests that Mediterranean and subtropical styles of vegetation existed in these polar regions in Cretaceous times. Unusually, these plants share the habit of seasonal leaf loss, probably in response to low winter light levels and temperatures. The Cretaceous world shows no evidence of polar ice caps and it seems probable that even at high latitudes, during the summer season at least, temperatures were extremely mild. Under such circumstances, it is highly likely that herbivorous dinosaurs migrated north or south, depending upon the season, to take advantage of rich pastures. As a result, discovery of their fossil remains at very high Mesozoic latitudes may reflect their migratory range rather than polar residency.

Ecological considerations

Measuring Mesozoic community structure was one of Bakker's most innovative suggestions in his search for proxies for dinosaurian physiology. The idea is beguilingly simple: endothermic and ectothermic animals require differing amounts of food in order to survive – these amounts reflect the basic 'running costs' associated with being either an endotherm or ectotherm. Endotherms, such as mammals and birds, have high running costs because much of the food that they eat (in excess of 80%) is burned to produce body heat. By contrast, ectotherms need far less food because very little is used to generate body heat. As a rough guide, ectotherms need about 10%, sometimes much less, of the food requirements of similarly sized endotherms.

Based on this observation, and an understanding that the general economy of Nature tends to keep supply and demand more or less in balance, Bakker suggested that censuses of fossil communities might indicate the balance between predator and prey, and by implication the physiology of these animals. He combed through museum collections to gather the data he needed. This included data from ancient (Palaeozoic) reptile, dinosaur (Mesozoic), and relatively more recent (Cenozoic) mammal communities. His results seemed encouraging: Palaeozoic reptile communities indicated a rough equivalence of predator and prey numbers; by contrast, dinosaur and Cenozoic mammal communities indicated a preponderance of prey animals and very small numbers of predators.

At first the scientific community was impressed with these results; however, considerable doubt now exists about the value of the original data. Using museum collections to estimate numbers of predators or prey is an exceedingly dubious exercise: there is no proof that the animals being counted lived together in the first instance; there are enormous biases in terms of what was (or was not) collected at the time; and all manner of assumptions are being made about what a predator will or will not eat; and, even if there was some sort of biological signal, it would surely only apply to the predator. Additionally, work on communities of living ectotherm predators and their prey has revealed that the predators may be as few as 10% of their potential prey numbers, mimicking the proportions seen in Bakker's supposedly endotherm communities.

This is an excellent example of a brilliant idea that sadly cannot be supported because the data simply will not yield results that are in any way meaningful scientifically.

Bone histology

Considerable attention has been directed toward understanding fine details of the internal structure of dinosaur bone. The mineral structure of dinosaur bone is generally unaffected by fossilization. As a result, it is often possible to create thin sections of bone that reveal the internal structure (histology) of the bone in amazing detail. Preliminary observations suggested that the bones of dinosaurs were closely similar in internal structure to those seen in living endothermic mammals, rather than those of modern ectotherms.

In general terms, the mammal and dinosaur bones revealed high levels of vascularization (they were very porous), while the ectotherm bones were poorly vascularized. The highly vascularized type of bone structure can arise in different ways. For example, one pattern of vascularization (fibrolamellar) reflects very rapid phases of bone growth. Another pattern (Haversian) represents a phase of strengthening of bone by remodelling that occurs later in the life of an individual.

What can be said is that many dinosaur remains show evidence of them having been able to grow quickly, and an ability to strengthen their bones by internal remodelling. Dinosaurs sometimes exhibit periodic interruptions in their pattern of growth (which mimics the intermittent pattern seen in the bones of living reptiles), but this style of growth is by no means uniform. Equally, and less probably, some endotherms (both bird and mammal) exhibit a style of bone structure (zonal) that displays very little vascularization, while living ectotherms can exhibit highly vascularized bone in parts of their skeletons. There are, surprisingly, no clear correlates between an animal's physiology and its internal bone structure.

Dinosaur physiology: an overview

The discussion above illustrates the range and variety of approaches that have been used in an attempt to investigate dinosaur metabolism.

Robert Bakker took an unquestioning stance when assessing the significance of the mammalian replacement by dinosaurs on land in the Early Jurassic. This pattern, he argued, could only be explained if dinosaurs were able to compete with his model of the 'superior' endothermic mammals: to do so, they simply had to be endothermic. Is this true? The answer is actually: no . . . not necessarily.

At the close of the Triassic and very beginning of the Jurassic, the world was one that we mammalian humans would not find particularly hospitable. Much of Pangaea at the time was affected by seasonal, but generally arid, conditions in which deserts became widespread globally. Such conditions of high temperatures and low rainfall exert selective pressures on endothermic and ectothermic metabolisms in very different ways.

Ectotherms, as argued above, need to eat less than endotherms and are therefore better able to survive times of low biological productivity. Reptiles have scaly skin that greatly resists water loss in dry, desert conditions; they also do not urinate but instead excrete a dry, pasty material (similar to bird droppings). High ambient temperatures suit ectotherms well because their internal chemistry can be maintained at optimum temperatures with relative ease. All in all, ectotherms, built in the classic reptilian mould, can be predicted to cope well with desert-like conditions.

Endotherms, such as mammals, are physiologically stressed in high-temperature conditions. Mammals are 'geared' to being able to lose heat to the environment from their bodies (their bodily thermostats maintain their temperature on average higher than normal environmental conditions) and adjust their physiology accordingly. When cold, mammals are able to reduce heat loss from the body by raising their fur to trap air and increase its insulatory efficiency, use 'shivering' to quickly generate extra muscular heat, or raise their basal metabolic rate. However, under conditions of high ambient temperature, the need to lose heat to the environment to prevent lethal overheating becomes vital. Evaporative cooling is one of the few options available; this is achieved either by panting or sweating through the skin surface. Both of these processes remove large volumes of water from the body. In desert conditions, losing water, which is in short supply, can prove fatal. To compound matters further, mammals remove the breakdown products of their metabolism from the body by urinating, which flushes wastes out of the body in a watery solution. In addition to the problems of heat load and water loss, mammals require large quantities of food to maintain their endothermic physiology. Deserts are areas of low productivity, so food supplies are restricted and not capable of sustaining large populations of endotherms.

Looked at from this purely environmental perspective, perhaps the Late Triassic/Early Jurassic world was unusual. It was a time when the environment probably favoured ectotherms and restricted early mammals to small size and primarily nocturnal niches. In deserts today, nearly all mammals (with the exception of those truly remarkable creatures known as camels) are small, exclusively nocturnal rodents and insectivores. They survive the extreme heat of the day by burrowing under the sand surface, where conditions are cooler and more damp, and they come out at night once the temperature has dropped and they can use their acute senses to find insect prey.

The striking aridity of the Late Triassic/Early Jurassic eventually ameliorated, as Pangaea began to disintegrate and shallow epicontinental seas spread across and between areas of land. The general climatic regime appears to have become extremely warm and wet, and these conditions prevailed across very broad latitudinal bands. It should be emphasized that there were no ice-covered polar regions throughout the time of the dinosaurs. The type of world we inhabit today is very unusual, when compared to much of the history of the Earth, in that it has both north and south poles covered in ice and consequently unusually narrowly confined latitudinal climatic bands. Under these relatively lush Jurassic conditions, productivity rose dramatically; major Jurassic coal deposits were laid down in areas where long-lived and densely forested areas existed. So it is perhaps not surprising to discover that the range and variety of dinosaurs surged during Jurassic times.

Dinosaur physiology: was it unique?

Dinosaurs are noteworthy as being large creatures; even medium-sized ones ranged between 5 and 10 metres in length, which is still very big by most standards – the average size of all mammals is probably about the size of a cat or small dog today. It is certainly true that no dinosaurs were mouse-sized (except as hatchlings).

Under some conditions, being large has advantages. Most notably, larger animals tend to lose heat to and gain heat from the environment very much more slowly than small ones. For example, adult crocodiles maintain a very stable internal body temperature day and night, whereas hatchlings exhibit a body temperature range that exactly mirrors the day and night changes. So, being dinosaur-sized means that your internal body temperature changes little over time. Being large also means that postural muscles need to work hard to prevent the body from collapsing under its own weight. This constant muscular 'work' generates significant quantities of energy (in the same way that we become 'flushed' with heat after muscular exercise), and this heat can assist in maintaining internal body temperature.

In addition to these advantages of size, we have seen that the probable agility as well as posture of dinosaurs, many with heads raised significantly above chest level, indicates the strong likelihood that they had highly efficient, fully divided hearts that were capable of rapidly circulating oxygen, food, and heat around the body, as well as removing harmful metabolism by-products. The fact that saurischian dinosaurs probably possessed a bird-like lung system further emphasizes their ability to provide the oxygen that their tissues needed during energetic, aerobic exercise.

Considering these factors alone, it seems very likely that dinosaurs possessed many of the attributes that we associate today with endothermy as seen in living mammals and birds. In addition, dinosaurs were typically large and therefore relatively thermally inert. They also lived during a time of constantly warm, non-seasonal, global climate.

It could be the case that dinosaurs were the happy inheritors of an ideal type of biology that enabled them to prosper in the unique climatic conditions that prevailed in the Mesozoic Era. But, however convincing this argument might seem at this point, it does not take into account one other crucial line of evidence that has emerged over the last few years: the intimacy of dinosaur–bird relationships.

Chapter 6
What if . . . birds *are* dinosaurs?

Following on from John Ostrom's inspired work in the 1970s, the anatomical evidence for a relationship between dinosaurs and birds is now so detailed that it is possible to reconstruct the stages by which a dromaeosaurian theropod might be transformed into an early bird.

Early small-sized theropods, such as *Compsognathus*, have a bird-like appearance – long, spindly legs; a long neck; and fairly small head with quite large, forward-pointing eyes – though they still retain obviously dinosaurian features, such as the clawed hands, teeth in the jaws, and a long, bulky tail.

Dromaeosaurian theropods

These bird-like dinosaurs exhibit a number of interesting anatomical changes to the basic theropod body plan. Some changes are quite subtle, but others are less so.

One notable feature is the 'thinning' of the tail: the tail becomes very narrow and stiffened by bundles of long, thin bones, the only flexible part being close to the hips (Figure 16, top). As argued earlier, this thin, pole-like tail may well have been valuable as a dynamic stabilizer to assist with the capture of fast-moving and elusive prey. However, this type of tail dramatically changed the pose of these animals because it was no longer a heavy, muscular cantilever for the front half of the body. If no other changes had been made to its posture, such a dinosaur would have been unbalanced and constantly pitch forward on to its nose!

To compensate for the loss of the heavy tail, the bodies of these theropods were subtly altered: the pubic bone, which marks the rearmost part of the gut and normally points forward and downward from each hip socket in theropods, was rotated backwards so that it lay parallel to the ischium (the other lower hip bone). Because of this change in orientation, the gut and associated organs could be swung backwards to lie beneath the hips. This change shifted the weight of the body backwards, and compensated for the loss of the heavy counterbalancing tail. This layout of hip bones, with the pubis rotated backward, is seen in living and fossil birds as well as maniraptoran theropods.

Another equally subtle way of compensating for the loss of the counterbalancing tail would be to shorten the chest in front of the hips, and this is also seen in these bird-like theropods. The chest also shows signs of being stiffened, and this probably reflects the predatory habits of these animals. The long arms and three-clawed hands were important for catching and subduing their prey and needed to be very powerful. The chest region was no doubt strengthened to help securely anchor the arms and shoulders to withstand the large forces associated with grappling and subduing prey. Birds also have a short, and greatly stiffened, chest region to withstand the forces associated with anchoring the powerful flight muscles.

At the front of the chest, between the shoulder joints, there is a V-shaped bone (which is in fact the fused clavicles, or collar bones – Figure 17) that acts as a spring-like spacer separating the shoulders, it also helped to anchor the shoulders in place while these animals were wrestling their prey. Birds also exhibit fused collar bones; they form the elongate 'wish bone', or furcula, that similarly acts as a mechanical spring that separates the shoulder joints during flapping flight.

The joints between the bones of the arm and hand were also modified so that they could be swung outward and downward with considerable speed and force to strike at prey in what has been called a 'raking' action. When not in use, the arms could be folded neatly against the body. The leverage for this system was also of considerable advantage to these creatures, because the arm muscles that powered this mechanism were located close to the chest and operated long tendons that ran down the arm to the hand (rather than having muscles positioned further out along the arm); this remote control system kept the weight of the body closer to the hips and helped to minimize the delicate problem of balance in these theropods. The arm-striking and arm-folding mechanism is closely similar to that employed by birds when opening and closing their wings during and after flight.

Archaeopteryx

The early bird-like fossil *Archaeopteryx* (Figure 16, bottom) exhibits many maniraptoran theropod features: the tail is a long and very thin set of vertebrae that anchored the tail feathers on either side; the hip bones are arranged with the pubis pointing backward and downward; at the front of the chest there is a boomerang-like furcula; the jaws are lined with small, spiky teeth, rather than a more typical bird-like horny beak; the arms are long, jointed so that they can be extended and folded just as in theropods, and the hands are equipped with three sharply clawed fingers that in their arrangement and proportions are identical to those seen in maniraptoran theropods.

Specimens of *Archaeopteryx* were preserved as fossils under exceptional circumstances that enabled an array of exquisitely delineated flight feather impressions to be seen. These are attached to the wings and along the sides of the tail and dictate that this

34. Restoration of the living *Archaeopteryx*

creature is defined as a bird: feathers are regarded as unique to birds, and therefore indicate its affinity beyond any question. This is one of the reasons why *Archaeopteryx* is considered to be such an important fossil, and why it has been the focus of this comparison. Had chance not led to the preservation of feathers in this instance, it is tempting to wonder how this creature might have been classified. It would very probably have been redescribed in recent years as an unusually small, dromaeosaurian theropod!

Chinese wonders

During the 1990s, explorations in quarries in Liaoning Province in north-eastern China began to yield some extraordinary, and extraordinarily well preserved, fossils of Early Cretaceous age. At first, these comprised beautifully preserved early birds such as *Confuciusornis*, and the skeletons included impressions of feathers, beaks, and claws. Then in 1996, a complete skeleton of a small theropod dinosaur, very similar in anatomy and proportions to the well known theropod *Compsognathus* (Figure 14), was described by Ji Qiang and Ji Shu'an. They named the dinosaur *Sinosauropteryx*. This dinosaur was remarkable because there was a fringe of filamentous structures along its backbone and across its body, suggesting some sort of covering to the skin that was akin to the 'pile' on a roughly made carpet; there was also evidence of soft tissues in the eye socket and in the region of the gut. It was clear that some small theropods had some type of body covering. These discoveries led to concerted efforts to find more such fossils at Liaoning; they began to appear with increasing regularity and ushered in some truly breathtaking revelations.

Shortly after *Sinosauropteryx* was discovered, another skeleton was revealed. This animal, named *Protoarchaeopteryx*, was the first to show the presence of true bird-like feathers attached to its tail and along the sides of its body, and its anatomy was much more similar to that of dromaeosaurians than *Sinosauropteryx*. Another discovery revealed an animal that was extremely similar to *Velociraptor*, but this time named *Sinornithosaurus* (again, apparently covered in a 'pile' of short filaments). Newer discoveries have included *Caudipteryx*, a large (turkey-sized), rather short-armed creature noted for a pronounced tuft of tail feathers and shorter fringes of feathers along its arms; smaller, heavily feathered dromaeosaurians; and in the spring of 2003 a quite remarkable 'four-winged' dromaeosaurian, *Microraptor*, was unveiled to the world. This latter creature was small and classically dromaeosaur-like, with the typically long, narrow tail, bird-like pelvis, long, grasping arms, and sharp rows of teeth lining its jaws. The tail was fringed by primary feathers and its body covered in downy ones. However, what was singularly impressive was the preservation along the arms of flight feathers forming *Archaeopteryx*-like wings and, very unexpectedly, similar wing-like fringes of feathers attached to the lower parts of the legs – hence the name 'four-wing'.

Such has been the avalanche of new, ever more startling discoveries from the quarries in Liaoning over such a short space of time that it is almost impossible to imagine what might be discovered next.

Birds, theropods, and the question of dinosaur physiology

The stunning new discoveries from Liaoning contribute importantly to the earlier discussion about the biology and physiology of dinosaurs; but, as ever, they do not answer quite as many questions as we would wish.

First and foremost, it is now clear that our Victorian predecessors were not correct: feathers do not, after all, make a bird. Various sorts of skin coverings appear to have been present on a wide range of theropod dinosaurs, ranging from a shaggy, filamentous type of covering, through downy, feather-like body coverings, to fully formed contour and flight feathers. The discoveries at Liaoning force us to wonder just how widespread such body coverings might have been, not only among theropods, but, perhaps, even in other dinosaur groups as well. Given the known distribution of body coverings, it is not unreasonable to ponder the probability of giants such as *Tyrannosaurus rex* (which was a theropod related to *Sinosauropteryx*) having some sort of epidermal covering – even if only as juveniles. Such tantalizing questions cannot be answered at present, and require the discovery of new geological deposits similar in quality of fossil preservation to those at Liaoning.

It is also quite obvious that a considerable diversity of feathered theropods and what we today recognize as genuine birds (ones with a well-developed flight apparatus) coexisted during Jurassic and Cretaceous times. *Archaeopteryx* is late Jurassic (155 Ma) in age and was clearly feathered and bird-like. However, we now know for certain that during the younger Cretaceous (c. 120 Ma) a multiplicity of these types of 'dinobirds', such as *Microraptor* and its relatives, existed alongside true birds. The sheer diversity, or biological exuberance, of these 'dinobirds' is rather bewildering, and to some extent obscures the evolutionary origins of the true birds that we see around today.

From a physiological perspective, however, the proof of the existence of theropod dinosaurs with some sort of insulatory covering points very conclusively toward the fact that these dinosaurs (at least) were genuine endotherms. There are two reasons for believing this:

i)   Many of these feathered dinosaurs were small-bodied (20–40 centimetres long) and, as we know, small animals have a relatively large surface area and lose body heat to the environment very quickly. Therefore insulation using filaments (which mimic the fur seen on the bodies of living mammals) and downy feathers are likely to have been a necessity if these creatures generated internal body heat.

ii) Equally, the possession of an outer insulatory layer to the skin would have made basking difficult, if not impossible, because the insulatory layer would have inhibited their ability to gain heat from the sun. Basking is the ectotherm's way of gaining body heat, so a furry or feathered lizard is a biological impossibility.

Birds from dinosaurs: an evolutionary commentary

The implications of these new discoveries are truly fascinating. It has already been argued, with logic and some force, that small theropod dinosaurs were highly active, fast-moving, and biologically 'sophisticated' animals. On this basis, they seemed reasonable candidates as potential endotherms; in a sense, our inferences about their way of life suggested that they had most to benefit from being endothermic. The Liaoning discoveries confirm that many of these highly active, bird-like dinosaurs were small animals. This is a crucial point, as small size puts greatest physiological stress on endotherms because a large percentage of internally generated body heat can be lost through the skin surface;

so small, active endotherms would be expected to insulate their bodies to reduce heat loss. Small theropod dinosaurs, therefore, evolved insulation to prevent heat loss because they were endotherms – not because they 'wanted' to become birds!

Liaoning discoveries indicate that various types of insulatory covering developed, most probably by subtle modifications to the growth patterns of normal skin scales; these ranged from hair-like filaments to full-blown feathers. It may well be that genuinely bird-like flight feathers did not evolve for the purposes of flight, but had a far more prosaic origin. Several of the 'dinobirds' from Liaoning seem to have tufts of feathers on the end of the tail (rather like a geisha's fan) and fringes of feathers along the arms, on the head, or running down the spine. Clearly preservational biases may also play a part in how and on which parts of the body these may be preserved. But for the present, it seems at least possible that feathers evolved as structures linked to the behaviour of these animals: providing recognition signals, perhaps, as in living birds, or being used as part of their mating rituals, long before any genuine flight function had developed.

In this context, gliding and flight, rather than being the *sine qua non* of avian origins, become later, 'add-on' benefits. Obviously, feathers have the potential for aerodynamic uses; just as with modern birds, the ability to jump and flutter may well have embellished 'dinobird' mating displays. For example, in the case of the small creature *Microraptor*, a combination of fringes of feathers along the arms, legs, and tail would have provided it with the ability to launch itself into the air from branches or equivalent vantage points. From just this sort of starting point, gliding and true flapping flight seem a comparatively short 'step' indeed.

Persistent problems

We should not, however, get too carried away with the scenario outlined above. Although the Liaoning discoveries are indeed incredibly important, offering, as they do, a richly detailed window on dinosaurian and avian evolution in the Cretaceous, they do not necessarily provide all the answers. One crucial point that must be remembered is that the quarries of Liaoning are Early Cretaceous in age, and their fossils are therefore considerably younger (by some 30 Ma at least) than the earliest well-preserved feathered dinosaur with highly developed and complex wings, *Archaeopteryx*. Whatever the path that led to the evolution of the first flying dinosaurs, and ultimately to birds, it was emphatically not via the extraordinary feathered dinosaurs from Liaoning. What we see at Liaoning is a snap shot of the evolutionary diversification of avian theropods (and some true birds), not the origin of birds: bird origins are still shrouded by sediments of Middle or possibly even Early Jurassic age – before *Archaeopteryx* ever fluttered to Earth. Everything that we know to date points to a very close relationship between theropod dinosaurs and early birds, but those crucial Early or Middle Jurassic theropods that were ancestral to *Archaeopteryx* are yet to be discovered. It is to be hoped that in future years some spectacular discoveries will be made that fill in this part of the story.

Chapter 5 concluded with the view that dinosaurs lived at a time in Earth history that favoured large-bodied, highly active creatures that were able to maintain a stable, high body temperature without most of the costs of being genuinely endothermic. The 'dinobirds' from Liaoning suggest that this view is wrong – small, insulated theropods simply had to be endothermic and their close relationship to birds, which we know are endothermic, simply reinforces the point.

My response to this is: well, yes and no. There is now little doubt that bird-like theropod dinosaurs were endotherms in a true sense. However, I do think that the arguments suggesting that the majority of more traditional dinosaurs were inertial homeotherms (their large body size enabled stable internal temperature) still hold. There is some evidence in support of my view to be found among living endotherms. Elephants, for example, have a much lower metabolic rate than mice – for exactly these reasons. Mice are small, lose heat rapidly to the environment, and have to maintain a high metabolic rate to replenish the heat loss. Elephants are large (generally dinosaur-sized) and have a stable internal body temperature due to their size, not just because they are endothermic. Indeed, being a large endotherm is, in part at least, a physiological challenge. For example, elephants suffer problems if they move around too quickly: their postural and leg muscles create a great deal of extra chemical heat, and they need to use their large, 'flappy' ears to help them to radiate heat rapidly to prevent fatal overheating.

Dinosaurs were on the whole super-large and their bodies would have been capable of maintaining a constant internal temperature; extrapolating from the elephant, it would not have been in dinosaurs' interests to be genuine endotherms, in a world that was in any case very warm. Having evolved physiologically as mass-homeotherms (having a stable internal body temperature that was made possible by large body size), the only group of dinosaurs that bucked the general dinosaurian trend toward large size and evolved into a small-bodied group were the dromaeosaurian theropods.

It is clear, from their anatomy alone, that dromaeosaurians were highly active and would have benefited from homeothermy, and their relatively large brains would have demanded a constant supply of oxygen and nutrients. Paradoxically, homeothermy cannot be maintained at small body size without an insulatory covering because of the unsustainable heat loss through the skin. The choice was stark and simple: small theropods had to either abandon their high-activity lifestyle and become conventionally reptilian, or boost internal heat production and become properly endothermic, avoiding heat loss by developing skin insulation. So, I propose that it is not a case of 'all or nothing'; most dinosaurs were basically mass-homeotherms that were able to sustain high activity levels without the full costs of mammalian or avian styles of endothermy; however, the small, and in particular the dromaeosaurian, theropods (and their descendants, the true birds) were obliged to develop full-blown endothermy and the associated insulatory covering.

Chapter 7

Dinosaur research: observation and deduction

In this chapter, a variety of lines of investigation are explored to reinforce the message that a multiplicity of approaches must be used if we are to comprehend the lives of fossil animals.

Dinosaur ichnology

Some aspects of dinosaur research have an almost sleuth-like quality to them, perhaps none more so than ichnology – the study of footprints.

> There is no branch of detective science which is so important and so much neglected as the art of tracing footsteps.
>
> (Conan Doyle, *The Study in Scarlet*, 1891)

The study of dinosaur footprints has a surprisingly long history. Some of the first to be collected and exhibited were found in 1802 in Massachusetts by the young Pliny Moody while ploughing a field. These and other large three-toed prints were eventually illustrated and described by Edward Hitchcock in 1836 as the tracks left by gigantic birds; some can still be seen in the Pratt Museum of Amherst College. From the mid-19th century onwards, tracks were discovered at fairly regular intervals in various parts of the world. With the development of an understanding of the anatomy of dinosaurs, and most particularly the shape of their feet, it was realized that the large 'bird-like' three-toed prints that were found in Mesozoic rocks belonged to dinosaurs rather than giant birds. Such tracks, though of local interest, were rarely regarded as of great scientific value. However, in recent years, largely prompted by the work of Martin Lockley of the University of Colorado at Denver, it has begun to be appreciated more widely that tracks may provide a great deal of information.

First, and most obviously, preserved tracks record the activities of *living* dinosaurs. Individual prints also record the overall shape of the foot and the number of toes, which can often help to narrow down the likely trackmaker, especially if dinosaur skeletons have been discovered in similarly aged rocks nearby. While individual prints may be intrinsically interesting, a series of tracks provides a record of how the creature was actually moving. They reveal the orientation of the feet as they contact the ground, the length of the stride, the width of the track (how closely the right and left feet were spaced); from this evidence, it is possible to reconstruct how the legs moved in a mechanical sense. Furthermore, taking observations using data from a wide range of living animals it has also proved possible to calculate the speeds at which animals leaving tracks were moving. These estimates are arrived at by simply measuring the size of the prints and length of each stride and making an estimate of the length of the leg. Although the latter might seem at first sight difficult to estimate with great accuracy, the actual size of the footprints has proved to be a remarkably good guide (judging by living animals), and in some instances foot and leg bones or skeletons of dinosaurs that lived at the time the tracks were made are known.

The shape of individual tracks may also reveal information relevant to deducing how such animals were moving: relatively flat, broad prints indicate that the whole foot was in contact with the ground for quite a long time, suggesting that it was moving relatively slowly; in other instances, the tracks may just show the tips of the

35. Parallel rows of tracks made by a group of sauropod dinosaurs as they travelled across a moist lowland plain

toes making contact with the ground – suggesting that the animal was quite literally sprinting on the tips of its toes.

Another interesting aspect of dinosaur tracks relates to the circumstances that led to them being preserved at all. Tracks will not be preserved on hard ground, instead it needs to be relatively soft and usually moist, and ideally of a muddy consistency. Once the prints have been made, it is then important that they are not greatly disturbed before they solidify; this can happen if the prints are buried quickly beneath another layer of mud, because the surface becomes baked hard in the sun, or through the rapid precipitation of minerals that form a kind of cement within the footprint layer. Very frequently, it is possible to deduce from details of the sediment in which the tracks were made exactly what the conditions were like when the dinosaur left its tracks. This can range from the degree to which the mud was disturbed by the feet of the animal and how deeply the feet sank into the sediment, to how the sediment seems to have responded to the movements of the foot. Sometimes it can be seen that a creature was moving up or down slopes simply from the way sediment is scuffed up in front of, or behind, the main footprint. Tracks left by dinosaurs can therefore offer a great deal of information about not only how dinosaurs moved, but the types of environments that they moved in.

The study of tracks can also reveal information about dinosaur behaviour. On rare occasions, multiple tracks of dinosaurs have been discovered. One famous example, recorded in the Paluxy River at Glen Rose in Texas, was revealed by a famous dinosaur footprint explorer named Roland T. Bird. Two parallel tracks were found at this site, one made by a huge brontosaur and the other by a large carnivorous dinosaur. The tracks seemed to show the big carnivore tracks converging on the brontosaur. At the intersection of the tracks, one print is missing, and Bird suspected that this indicated the point of attack. However, Lockley was able to show from maps of the track site that the brontosaurs (there were several) continued walking beyond the supposed point of attack; and, even though the large theropod was following the brontosaur (some of its prints overlap those of the brontosaur), there is no sign of a 'scuffle'. Very probably this predator was simply tracking potential prey animals by following at a safe distance. More convincing were some tracks observed by Bird at Davenport Ranch, also in Texas. Here he was able to log the tracks of 23 brontosaur-like sauropods walking in the same direction at the same time (Figure 35). This suggested very strongly that some dinosaurs moved around in herds. Herding or gregarious behaviour is impossible to deduce from skeletons, but tracks provide direct evidence.

Increased interest in dinosaur tracks in recent years has brought to light a number of potentially interesting avenues of research. Dinosaur tracks have sometimes been found in areas that have not yielded skeletal remains of dinosaurs, so tracks can help to fill in particular gaps in the known fossil record of dinosaurs. Interesting geological concepts have also emerged from a consideration of dinosaur track properties. Some of the large sauropodomorph dinosaurs (the brontosaurs referred to above) may have weighed as much as 20–40 tonnes in life. These animals would have exerted enormous forces on the ground when they walked. On soft substrate, the pressure from the feet of such dinosaurs would have distorted the earth at a depth of a metre or more beneath the surface – creating a series of 'underprints' formed as echoes of the original footprint on the surface. The spectre of 'underprints' means that some dinosaur tracks might be considerably over-represented in the fossil record if a single print can be replicated through numerous 'underprints'.

If herds of such enormous creatures trampled over areas, as they certainly did at Davenport Ranch, then they also had the capacity to greatly disturb the earth beneath – pounding it up and destroying its normal sedimentary structure. This relatively recently recognized phenomenon has been named 'dinoturbation'. 'Dinoturbation' might be a geological phenomenon, but it hints at another distinctly biological effect linked to dinosaur activities that may or may not be measurable over time. That is the potential evolutionary and ecological impact of dinosaurs on terrestrial communities at large. Great herds of multitonne dinosaurs moving across a landscape had the potential to utterly devastate the local ecology. We are aware that elephants today are capable of causing considerable damage to the African savannah because of the way that they can tear up and knock down mature trees. What might a herd of 40-tonne brontosaurs have done? And did this type of destructive activity have an effect upon the other animals and plants living at the time; can we identify or measure such impacts in the long term, and were they important in the evolutionary history of the Mesozoic?

Coprolites

Another slightly less romantic branch of palaeobiological investigation focuses on the dung of animals such as dinosaurs. This material is refered to as coprolites (*copros* means dung, *lithos* means stone), and their study has a surprisingly long and relatively illustrious history. The recognition of the importance of preserved dung dates back to the work of William Buckland of Oxford University (the man who described the first dinosaur, *Megalosaurus*). A pioneering geologist from the first half of the 19th century, Buckland spent considerable time collecting and studying rocks and fossils from his native area around Lyme Regis in Dorset, including fossil marine reptiles. Alongside these, Buckland noted large numbers of distinctive pebbles that often had a faint spiral shape. On closer inspection, breaking them open and looking at polished sections, Buckland was able to identify shiny fish scales, bones, and the sharp hooks of belemnite (a cephalopod mollusc) tentacles in great concentrations. He concluded that these stones were most probably the lithified excreta of the predatory reptiles found in the same rocks. Clearly, though at first sight somewhat distasteful, the study of coprolites had the potential to reveal evidence concerning the diet of the once-living creature that would not otherwise be obtainable.

As was the case with footprints, the question 'who did this?', though obviously amusing, can present significant problems. Occasionally, coprolites, or indeed gut contents, have been preserved inside the bodies of some fossil vertebrates (notably fish); however, it has been difficult to connect coprolite fossils to specific dinosaurs or even groups of dinosaurs. Karen Chin of the US Geological Survey has devoted herself to the study of coprolites and has had singular difficulty in reliably identifying dinosaur coprolites – until quite recently.

In 1998, Chin and colleagues were able to report the discovery of what they referred to in the title of their article as 'A *king*-sized theropod coprolite'. The specimen in question was discovered in Maastrichtian (latest Cretaceous) sediments in Saskatchewan and comprised a rather nobbly lump of material, over 40 centimetres long, that had a volume of approximately 2.5 litres. Immediately around and inside the specimen were broken fragments of bone, and a finer, sand-like powder of bone material was present throughout the mass. Chemical analysis of the specimen confirmed that it had very high levels of calcium and phosphorous, confirming a high concentration of bone material. Histological thin sections of the fragments further confirmed the cellular structure of bone and that the most likely prey items that had been digested were dinosaurian; as suspected, this specimen was most likely a large carnivore's coprolite. Surveying the fauna known from the rocks in this area, the only creature that was large enough to have been able to pass a coprolite of these dimensions was the large theropod *Tyrannosaurus rex* ('king' of the dinosaurs). Examination of the bone fragments preserved in the coprolite showed that this animal had been able to pulverize the bones of its prey in its mouth, and that the most likely prey was a juvenile ceratopian ornithischian (from the structure of the bone in the histological sections). The fact that not all the bone had been digested in this coprolite indicated that the material had moved through the gut with considerable speed, which could be used by some as evidence that *T. rex* was perhaps a hungry endotherm.

Dinosaur pathologies

The confirmation of a diet of meat in *T. rex* is clearly not entirely unexpected, given the overall anatomy of such theropods. However, an interesting pathological consequence of a diet rich in red meat has also been detected in the skeleton of *Tyrannosaurus*.

'Sue', the large skeleton of *Tyrannosaurus rex* now on display at the Field Museum in Chicago, is of interest because of the presence of various pathological features. One of its finger bones (metacarpals) exhibits some characteristic, smoothly rounded pits at the joint with its first finger bone; these were subjected to detailed examination by modern-day pathologists as well as palaeontologists. The palaeontologists discovered that other tyrannosaurs also exhibit such lesions, but that these are quite rare in museum collections. The pathologist was able to confirm, following detailed comparison with pathologies from living reptiles and birds, that the lesions were the result of gout. This illness, also known in humans, generally affects the feet and hands, and is extremely painful, causing swelling and inflammation of the areas involved. It is caused by the deposition of urate crystals around the joints. Although gout can be a result of dehydration or of kidney failure, a factor in humans is diet: ingesting food rich in purine, a chemical found in red meat. So, *Tyrannosaurus* not only looked like a meat-eater, its faeces prove it, and so does one of the diseases it suffered from.

'Sue' also displays a large number of more conventional pathologies. These are the tell-tale remains of past injuries. When bones are broken during life, they have the capacity to heal themselves. Although modern surgical techniques enable repair of broken bones with considerable precision, in Nature the broken ends of the bone do not usually align themselves precisely, and a callous forms around the area where the ends of bone meet. Such imperfections in the repair process leave marks on the skeleton that can be detected after death. It is clear that 'Sue' suffered a number of injuries during 'her' life. On one occasion, 'she' experienced a major trauma to the chest, which exhibits several clearly broken and repaired ribs. In addition, 'her' spine and tail show a number of breakages that, again, healed during life.

The surprising aspect of these observations is that an animal such as *T. rex* was clearly able to survive periods of injury and sickness. It might be predicted that a large predator such as *T. rex* would become extremely vulnerable and therefore potential prey itself once it was injured. That this did not happen (at least in the instance of 'Sue') suggests either that such animals were extraordinarily durable and therefore not unduly affected by quite serious trauma, or that these dinosaurs may have lived in socially cohesive groups that might have acted cooperatively on occasion to assist an injured individual.

Other pathologies have also been noted in various dinosaurs. These range from destructive bone lesions resulting from periodontal abscesses (in the case of jaw bones), or septic arthritis and chronic osteomyelitis in other parts of the skull or skeleton. One particularly unpleasant example of long-term infection of a leg wound was recorded in a small ornithopod. The partial skeleton of this animal was discovered in Early Cretaceous sediments in south-eastern Australia. The hindlimbs and pelvis were well preserved, but the lower part of the left leg was grossly distorted and shortened (Figure 36). Although the original cause of the subsequent infection could not be proved, it was suspected that the animal may have received a severe bite on the shin close to the knee of its left leg. As a result, the fossilized bones of the shin (tibia and fibula) were severely overgrown by a huge, irregular, callous-like mass of bone.

Examination and X-radiography of the fossil bone revealed that the site of the original injury must have become infected, but that rather than remaining localized the infection spread down the marrow cavity of the shin bone, partially destroying the bone as it went. As the infection spread, extra bony tissue was added to the exterior of the bone as if the body was trying to create its own 'splint' or support. It is clear that the animal's immune system was unable to prevent the continued spread of infection, and large abscesses formed beneath the outer bony sheath; the pus from these must have leaked through from the leg bones and may have run out on to the surface of the skin as a sore. Judging by the amount of bone growth around the site of infection, it seems likely that the animal

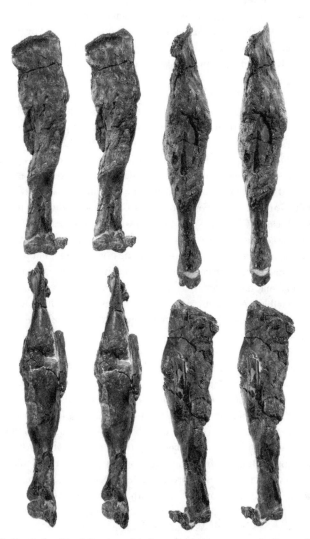

36. Septic fossilized dinosaur shin bones have become grossly distorted

lived for as much as a year, while suffering from this horribly crippling injury, before it finally succumbed. The preserved skeleton shows no other sign of pathological infection, and there is no indication of tooth marks or other scavenging activity because its bones were not scattered.

Tumours have only rarely been recognized in dinosaur bones. The most obvious drawback with trying to study the frequency of cancers in dinosaurs has been the need to destroy dinosaurian bone in order to make histological sections – obviously something that has little appeal to museum curators. Recently, Bruce Rothschild has developed a technique for scanning dinosaur bones using X-rays and fluoroscopy. The technique is limited to bones less than 28 centimetres in diameter, and for this reason he surveyed large numbers (over 10,000) of dinosaur vertebrae. The vertebrae came from representatives of all the major dinosaur groups from a large number of museum collections. He discovered that cancers were not only very rare (<0.2% to 3%) but also limited exclusively to hadrosaurs.

Quite why tumours should be so restricted is puzzling. Rothschild was moved to wonder whether the diets of hadrosaurs may have had a bearing on this epidemiology. Rare discoveries of 'mummified' carcasses of hadrosaurs show accumulations of material in the gut that include considerable quantities of conifer tissue; these plants contain high concentrations of tumour-inducing chemicals. Whether this provides evidence either for a genetic predisposition to cancer among hadrosaurs, or for environmental induction (a mutagenic diet), is entirely speculative at present.

Isotopes

Another branch of science known as geochemistry has been using radioactive isotopes of oxygen, particularly oxygen-16 and oxygen-18, and their proportions in chemicals (carbonates) found in the shells of microscopic marine organisms, to estimate the temperature of ancient oceans, and therefore larger-scale climatic conditions. Basically, the understanding is that the higher the proportion of oxygen-18 (compared to oxygen-16) locked into the chemicals of the shells of these organisms, the colder the temperature of the ocean in which the organisms originally lived.

In the early 1990s, a palaeontologist, Reese Barrick, and a geochemist, William Showers, joined forces to see if it might be possible to do the same for the chemicals in bones – particularly the oxygen that forms part of the phosphate molecule in bone minerals. They first applied this approach to some known vertebrates (cows and lizards) by taking samples of bones from different parts of the body (ribs, legs, and tail) and measured the oxygen isotope proportions. Their results showed that for the endothermic mammal (cow) there was very little difference in the body temperature between the bones of the legs and ribs; as might be expected, the animal had a constant body temperature. In the lizard, however, the tail was between 2 and 9°C lower than its ribs; the ectotherm did not have such an even distribution of body heat, with the peripheral parts on average cooler than the body core.

Barrick and Showers then performed a similar analysis on various bones from a well-preserved *T. rex* skeleton collected in Montana. Drilled samples from ribs, leg, toe, and tail bones revealed a rather mammal-like result: the oxygen isotope ratios differed very little, indicating that the body had a fairly even temperature throughout. This was used to promote further the idea that dinosaurs were not only homeothermic but also that they were endothermic. More recent work by these authors seems to confirm their basic finding, and has extended this observation to a range of other dinosaurs, including hadrosaurs.

As is often the case, these results generated a lively discussion. There were concerns that the bones may have been chemically altered during fossilization, which would render the isotopic signals meaningless, and physiologically minded palaeobiologists were far from convinced about what the result meant: a homeothermic signal is consistent with the idea that most dinosaurs were large-bodied mass-homeotherms (Chapter 6) and gives no conclusive evidence of endo- or ectothermy.

This is clearly an interesting line of inquiry; the results are not yet conclusive but provide the grounds for future research.

Dinosaur research: the scanning revolution

The steady improvement in technological resources, as well as their potential to be used to answer palaeobiological questions, has manifested in a number of distinct areas in recent years. A few of these will be examined in the following section; they are not without their limitations and pitfalls, but in some instances questions may now be asked that could not have been dreamt of 10 years ago.

One of the most anguished dilemmas faced by palaeobiologists is the desire to explore as much of any new fossil as possible, but at the same time to minimize the damage caused to the specimen by such action. The discovery of the potential for X-rays to create images on photographic film of the interior of the body has been of enormous importance to medical science. The more recent revolution in medical imaging through the development of CT (computed tomography) and MRI (magnetic resonance imaging) techniques that are linked directly to powerful data-processing computers has resulted in the ability to create three-dimensional images that allow researchers to see inside objects such as the human body or other complex structures that would only normally be possible after major exploratory surgery.

The potential to use CT scanning to see inside fossils was rapidly appreciated. One of the leaders in the field is Tim Rowe, with his team based at the University of Texas in Austin. He has managed to set up one of the finest fossil-dedicated, high-resolution CT scanning systems and, as we shall see below, has put it to some extremely interesting uses.

Investigating hadrosaurian crests

One obvious use of CT scanning can be demonstrated by referring to the extravagant range of crests seen on some hadrosaurian ornithopods. These dinosaurs were very abundant in Late Cretaceous times and have remarkably similarly shaped bodies; they only really differ in the shape of their headgear, but the reason for this difference has been a long-standing puzzle. When the first 'hooded' dinosaur was described in 1914, it was considered likely that these were simply interesting decorative features. However, in 1920 it was discovered that these 'hoods', or crests, were composed of thin sheaths of bone that enclosed tubular cavities or chambers of considerable complexity.

Theories to explain the purpose of these crests abounded from the 1920s onwards. The very earliest claimed that the crest provided an attachment area for ligaments running from the shoulders to the neck that supported the large and heavy head. From then on, ideas ranged from their use as weapons; that they carried highly developed organs of smell; that they were sexually specific (males had crests and females did not); and, the most far-sighted, that the chambers might have served as resonators, as seen in modern birds. During the 1940s, there was a preference for aquatic theories: that they formed an air-lock to prevent water flooding the lungs when these animals fed on underwater weeds.

Most of the more outlandish suggestions have been abandoned, either because physically impossible or they do not accord with the known anatomy. What has emerged is that the crests probably performed a number of interrelated functions of a mainly social/sexual type. They probably provided a visual social recognition system for individual species; and, in addition, some elaboration of the crests undoubtedly served a sexual display purpose. A small number of hadrosaur crests were sufficiently robust to have been used either in flank or head-butting activities as part of pre-mating rituals or male–male rivalry competitions. Finally, the chambers and tubular areas associated with the crests or facial structure are thought to have functioned as resonators. Again, this presumed vocal ability (found today in birds and crocodiles) can be linked to aspects of social behaviour in these dinosaurs.

One of the greatest problems associated with the resonator theory was gaining direct access to skull material that would allow detailed reconstruction of the air passages within the crest, without breaking open prized and carefully excavated specimens. CT techniques made such internal investigations feasible. For example, some new material of the very distinctively crested hadrosaur *Parasaurolophus tubicen* was collected from Late Cretaceous sediments in New Mexico. The skull was reasonably complete, well preserved, and included a long, curved crest. It was CT scanned along the length of the crest, then the scans were digitally processed so that the space inside the crest, rather than the crest itself, could be imaged. The rendered version of the interior cavity revealed an extraordinary degree of complexity. Several parallel, narrow tubes looped tightly within the crest, creating the equivalent of a cluster of trombones! There is now little doubt that the crest cavities in animals like *Parasaurolophus* were capable of acting as resonators as part of their vocal system.

Soft tissues: hearts of stone?

In the late 1990s, a new partial skeleton of a medium-sized ornithopod was discovered in Late Cretaceous sandstones in South Dakota. Part of the skeleton was eroded away, but what remained was extraordinarily well preserved, with evidence of some of the soft tissues, such as cartilage, which are normally lost during fossilization, still visible. During initial preparation of the specimen, a large ferruginous (iron-rich) nodule was discovered in the centre of the chest. Intrigued by this structure, the researchers obtained permission to CT scan a major part of the skeleton using a large veterinary hospital scanner. The results from these scans were intriguing.

The ferruginous nodule appeared to have distinctive anatomical features, and there appeared to be associated nearby structures. The researchers interpreted these as indicating that the heart and some associated blood vessels had been preserved within the nodule. The nodule appeared to show two chambers (interpreted by the researchers as representing the original ventricles of the heart); a little above these was a curved, tube-like structure that they interpret as an aorta (one of the main arteries leaving the heart). On this basis, they went on to suggest that this showed that dinosaurs of this type had a very bird-like, fully divided heart, which supported the increasing conviction that dinosaurs were generally highly active, aerobic animals (see Chapter 6).

As early as 1842, and the extraordinarily prophetic speculations of Richard Owen, it had been supposed that dinosaurs, crocodiles, and birds had a relatively efficient four-chambered (i.e. fully divided) heart. On that basis, this discovery is not so startling. What is astonishing is the thought that the general shape of the soft tissues of the heart of this particular dinosaur might have been preserved through some freak circumstance of fossilization.

Soft tissue preservation is known to occur under some exceptional conditions in the fossil record; these generally comprise a mixture of very fine sediments (muds and clays) that are capable of preserving the impressions of soft tissues. Also, soft tissues, or rather their chemically replaced remnants, can be preserved by chemical precipitation, usually in the absence of oxygen. Neither of these conditions apply to the ornithopod skeleton described above. The specimen was found in coarse sandstone, and under conditions that would have been oxygen-rich, so from a simple geochemical perspective, conditions would appear to be very unlikely to preserve soft tissues of any type.

Not surprisingly, the observations made by the researchers have been challenged. Ironstone nodules are commonly reported in these deposits and are frequently found associated with dinosaur bones. The sedimentary conditions, the chemical environment in which the structures might have been preserved, and the interpretation of all the supposedly heart-like features have been contested. At present, the status of this specimen is therefore uncertain, but whatever else is claimed, if these features are simply those of an ironstone nodule, then it is extraordinary that they are so heart-like.

Fake 'dinobirds': forensic palaeobiology

In 1999 an article appeared in the *National Geographic* magazine that highlighted the similarities between dinosaurs and birds that had been revealed by the new discoveries made in Liaoning Province, China. It brought to light another new and exciting specimen that was named *Archaeoraptor*, and was represented by a nearly complete skeleton that seemed as good an intermediate 'dinobird' as one could imagine. The animal had very bird-like wings and chest bones, yet retained rather theropod-like head, legs, and the long stiffened tail.

The specimen was initially fêted by *National Geographic* through public events. However, the specimen soon became dogged by controversy. It had been bought by a museum based in Utah at a fossil fair in Tucson, Arizona, even though it evidently came from China. This is very unusual because the Chinese government regards all fossils of scientific value as the property of China.

The specimen came to be regarded with suspicion by the scientific community: the front half of the body was almost *too* bird-like compared to the theropod-like legs and tail. The surface of limestone upon which this specimen was preserved was also

A. X-Ray image of the fossil

Model Key
Relative density
☐ bone

▨ slab materials

■ air

Map Key
Bones
■ associated bird bones

■ unverifiable
'attached' bones

Associated pieces
1a-w associated pieces
lying in natural position

37. The fake *'Archaeoraptor'* on its slab of rock

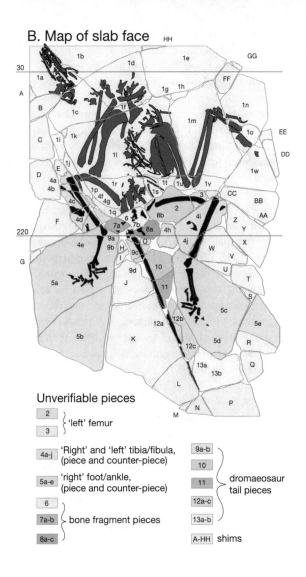

B. Map of slab face

Unverifiable pieces

2
3
} 'left' femur

4a-j   'Right' and 'left' tibia/fibula, (piece and counter-piece)

5a-e   'right' foot/ankle, (piece and counter-piece)

6
7a-b } bone fragment pieces
8a-c

9a-b
10
11
12a-c
13a-b
} dromaeosaur tail pieces

A-HH   shims

unusual, it consisted of a crazy-paving-like series of small slabs held together by a lot of filler (see Figure 37). Within a relatively short period of time, it was declared to be a probable fake – possibly manufactured to order from assorted spare parts collected in Liaoning. Amid the general air of concern, the curator of the Utah museum contacted two palaeontologists who had worked on these Chinese forms, Philip Currie of the Royal Tyrell Museum, Alberta, and Xu Xing of Beijing, China; and Tim Rowe was contacted at Texas to see if he could CT scan and verify the nature of this fossil.

By an amazing coincidence, Xu, on returning to China, located a piece of rock from Liaoning containing most of a dromaeosaur theropod. After studying this specimen, he became convinced that the tail of this fossil was the matching counterpart to the one he had recently seen on *Archaeoraptor*. Returning to Washington, and the office of *National Geographic*, Xu was able to place his recently discovered fossil against the *Archaeoraptor* specimen and demonstrate that the original *Archaeoraptor* block was without doubt a composite consisting of *at least* two different animals (the front half being part of a genuine bird, the back half being that of a dromaeosaur theropod).

Alerted to this, Rowe was able to study the CT scans that he made of the original *Archaeoraptor* slab in detail. CT cannot distinguish genuine from fraudulent fossils. However, the accuracy of the three-dimensional images of each portion of the slab allowed precise comparison of each piece of the specimen. It became clear that a partial bird fossil formed the main part of the slab, to this had been added the leg bones and feet of a theropod dinosaur. Rowe and his colleagues were able to show that only one leg bone and foot had been used. In this instance, the part and counterpart had been split apart to make a pair of legs and feet! Finally, the tail of the theropod had been added; and to complete the 'picture', additional pieces of paving and filler were added to create a more visually pleasing rectangular ensemble.

These dramatic revelations have had no effect whatever on the debate concerning dinosaur-bird relationships. What they do point to are some unfortunate facts. In China, where poorly paid labourers have helped to excavate some truly wondrous fossils, they have clearly developed a good knowledge of anatomy and an understanding of the sorts of creatures that scientists are looking for. These workers also realize that there is a thriving market in such fossils, which will bring them far better financial rewards if they can sell them to dealers outside China.

Dinosaur mechanics: how *Allosaurus* fed

Computed tomography has clearly proved to be a very valuable aid to palaeobiological investigations because it has this ability to see inside objects in an almost magical way. Some technologically innovative ways of using CT imaging have been developed by Emily Rayfield and colleagues, at the University of Cambridge. Using CT images, sophisticated computer software, and a great deal of biological and palaeobiological information, it has proved possible to investigate how dinosaurs may have functioned as living creatures.

As with the case of *Tyrannosaurus*, we know in very general terms that *Allosaurus* (Figure 31) was a predatory creature and probably fed on a range of prey living in Late Jurassic times. Sometimes tooth marks or scratches may be found on fossil bones and these can be quite literally lined up against the teeth in the jaws of an allosaur as a form of 'proof' of the guilty party. But what does such evidence tell us? The answer is: not as much as we might like. We cannot be sure if the tooth marks were left by a scavenger feeding off an already dead animal, or whether the animal that left the tooth marks was the real killer; equally, we cannot tell what style of predator an allosaur might have been: did it run down its prey after a long chase, or did it lurk and pounce? Did it have a devastating bone-crushing bite, or was it more of a cut and slasher?

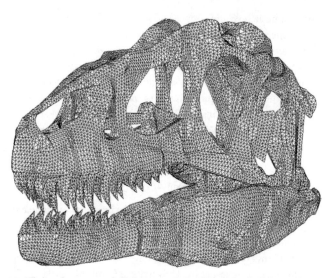

38. Finite-element modelled image of an *Allosaurus* skull derived from a CT scan

Rayfield was able to obtain CT scan data created from an exceptionally well-preserved skull of the Late Jurassic theropod *Allosaurus*. High-resolution scans of the skull were used to create a very detailed three-dimensional image of the entire skull. However, rather than simply creating a beautiful hologram-like representation of the skull, Rayfield converted the image data into a three-dimensional 'mesh'. The mesh consisted of a series of point coordinates (rather like the coordinates on a topographic map), each point was linked to its immediate neighbours by short 'elements'. This created what in engineering terms is known as a finite element map of the entire skull (Figure 38): nothing quite as complicated as this had ever been attempted before.

The remarkable property of this type of model is that with the appropriate computer and software it is possible to record, on the finite element map, the material properties of the skull bones, for example the strength of skull bone, of tooth enamel, or of cartilage on the joints between bones. In this way, each 'element' can be prompted to behave as though it were a piece of real skull, and each element is linked to its neighbours as an integrated unit, as it would be in life.

Having mapped the virtual skull of this dinosaur, it was then necessary to work out how powerful its jaw muscles were in life. Using clay, Rayfield was able to quite literally model the jaw muscles of this dinosaur. Once she had done this, she was able to calculate from their dimensions – their length, girth, and angle of attachment to the jaw bones – the amount of force that they could generate. To ensure that these calculations were as realistic as possible, two sets of force estimates were generated: one based on the view that dinosaurs like this one had a rather crocodile-like (ectotherm) physiology, the other assumed an avian/mammalian (endotherm) physiology.

Using these sets of data, it was then possible to superimpose these forces on the finite element model of the *Allosaurus* skull and quite literally 'test' how the skull would respond to maximum bite forces, and how these would be distributed within the skull. The experiments were intended to probe the construction and shape of the skull, and the way it responded to stresses associated with feeding.

What emerged was fascinating. The skull was extraordinarily strong (despite all the large holes over its surface that might be thought to have weakened it significantly). In fact, the holes proved to be an important part of the strength of the skull. When the virtual skull was tested until it began to 'yield' (that is to say, it was subjected to forces that were beginning to fracture its bones), it was found to be capable of withstanding up to 24 times the force that the jaw muscles could exert when they were biting as hard as 'allosaurianly' possible.

What became obvious from this experimentation was that the

allosaur skull was hugely over-engineered. Natural selection usually provides a 'safety factor' in the design of most skeletal features: a sort of trade-off between the amount of energy and materials needed to build that part of the skeleton and its overall strength under normal conditions of life. That 'safety factor' varies, but is generally in the range of 2–5 times the forces normally experienced during normal life activities. To have the skull of *Allosaurus* built with a 'safety factor' of 24 seemed ludicrous. Re-examination of the skull, and a rethink about its potential methods of feeding, led to the following realization: the lower jaw was actually quite 'weak' in the way it was constructed, so the animal probably did have a genuinely weak bite, compared to its overall skull strength. This suggested that the skull was constructed to withstand very large forces (in excess of 5 tonnes) for other reasons. The most obvious was that the skull may have been used as the principal attack weapon – as a chopper. These animals may well have lunged at their prey with the jaws opened very wide, and then slammed their head downward against their prey in a devastating, slashing blow. With the weight of the body behind this movement, and the resistance of the prey animal, the skull would need to be capable of withstanding short-term, but extremely high, loads.

Once the prey had been subdued following the first attack, the jaws could then be used to bite off pieces of flesh in the conventional way, but this might reasonably have been aided by using the legs and body to assist with tugs at resistant pieces of meat, again loading the skull quite highly through forces generated by the neck, back, and leg muscles.

In this particular analysis, it has been possible to gain an idea of *how* feeding may have been achieved in allosaurs in ways that until a few years ago would have been unimaginable. Yet again, the interplay between new technologies and different branches of science (in this instance engineering design) can be used to probe palaeobiological problems and generate new and interesting observations.

Ancient biomolecules and tissues

I cannot finish this chapter without mentioning the *Jurassic Park* scenario: discovering dinosaur DNA, using modern biotechnology to reconstitute that DNA, and using this to bring the dinosaur back to life.

There have been sporadic reports of finding fragments of dinosaur DNA in the scientific literature over the past decade, and then using PCR (polymerase chain reaction) biotechnology to amplify the fragments so that they can be studied more easily. Unfortunately, for those who wish to believe in the Hollywood-style scenario, absolutely none of these reports have been verified, and in truth it is exceedingly unlikely that any genuine dinosaur DNA will ever be isolated from dinosaur bone. It is simply the case that DNA is a long and complex biomolecule which degrades over time in the absence of the metabolic machinery that will maintain and repair it, as occurs in living cells. The chances of any such material surviving unaltered for over 65 million years while it is buried in the ground (and subject there to all the contamination risks presented by micro-organisms and other biological and chemical sources, and ground water) are effectively zero.

All reports of dino-DNA to date have proved to be records of contaminants. In fact the only reliable fossil DNA that has been identified is far more recent, and even these discoveries have been made possible because of unusual preservational conditions. For example, brown bear fossils whose remains are dated back to about 60,000 years have yielded short strings of mitochondrial DNA – but these fossils had been frozen in permafrost since the animals died, providing the best chance of reducing the rate of degradation of these molecules. Dinosaur remains are of course 1,000 times more ancient than those of arctic brown bears. Although it might be possible to identify some dinosaur-like genes in the DNA of living birds, regenerating a dinosaur is beyond the bounds of science.

One final, but extremely interesting, set of observations concerns the analysis of the appearance and chemical composition of the interior of some tyrannosaur bones from Montana. Mary Schweitzer and colleagues from North Carolina State University were given access to some remarkably well preserved *T. rex* bones collected by Jack Horner (the real-life model for 'Dr Alan Grant' in the film *Jurassic Park*). Detailed examination of the skeletal remains suggested that there had been minimal alteration of the internal structure of the long bones; indeed, so unaltered were they that the individual bones of the tyrannosaur had a density that was consistent with that of modern bones that had simply been left to dry.

Schweitzer was looking for ancient biomolecules, or at least the remnant chemical signals that they might have left behind. Having extracted material from the interior of the bones, this was powdered and subjected to a broad range of physical, chemical, and biological analyses. The idea behind this approach was not only to have the best chance of 'catching' some trace, but also to have a range of semi-independent support for the signal, if it emerged. The burden really is upon the researcher to find some positive proof of the presence of such biomolecules; the time elapsed since death and burial, and the overwhelming probability that any remnant of such molecules has been completely destroyed or flushed away, seem to be overwhelming. Nuclear magnetic resonance and electron spin resonance revealed the presence of molecular residues resembling haemoglobin (the primary chemical constituent of red blood cells); spectroscopic analysis and HPLC (high performance liquid chromatography) generated data that was also consistent with the presence of remnants of the haeme structure. Finally, the dinosaur bone tissues were flushed with solvents to extract any remaining protein fragments; this extract was then injected into laboratory rats to see if it would raise an immune response – and it did! The antiserum created by the rats reacted positively with purified avian and mammalian haemoglobins. From this set of analyses, it seems very probable that chemical remnants of dinosaurian haemoglobin compounds were preserved in these *T. rex* tissues.

Even more tantalizingly, when thin sections of portions of bone were examined microscopically, small, rounded microstructures could be identified in the vascular channels (blood vessels) within the bone. These microstructures were analysed and found to be notably iron-rich compared to the surrounding tissues (iron being a principal constituent of the haeme molecule). Also the size and general appearance was remarkably reminiscent of avian nucleated blood cells. Although these structures are not actual blood cells, they certainly seem to be the chemically altered 'ghosts' of the originals. Quite how these structures have survived in this state for 65 Ma is a considerable puzzle.

Schweitzer and her co-workers have also been able to identify (using immunological techniques similar to the one mentioned above) biomolecular remnants of the 'tough' proteins known as collagen (a major constituent of natural bone, as well as ligaments and tendons) and keratin (the material that forms scales, feathers, hair, and claws).

Although these results have been treated with considerable scepticism by the research community at large – and rightly so, for the reasons elaborated above – nevertheless, the range of scientific methodologies employed to support their conclusions, and the exemplary caution with which these observations were announced, represent a model of clarity and application of scientific methodologies in this field of palaeobiology.

Chapter 8
The future of research on the past

K-T extinctions: the end of dinosaurs?

Since the early decades of the 19th century, it had been known that different groups of organisms dominate different periods of Earth history. One of the more notable groups was the dinosaurs, and there was a steady reinforcement from palaeontological surveys of the idea that none were to be found in rocks younger than the end of the Cretaceous period (approximately 65 Ma). In fact, it came to be recognized that the very end of the Cretaceous Period, leading into the Tertiary Period (now universally referred to as the K-T boundary) marked a major time of change. Many species became extinct and were replaced in the Early Tertiary by a diversity of new forms: the K-T boundary therefore seemed to represent a major punctuation in life and consequently a mass-extinction event. The types of species that became extinct at this time included the fabled dinosaurs on land, of which there were many different varieties by Late Cretaceous times; a multiplicity of sea creatures, ranging from giant marine reptiles (mosasaurs, plesiosaurs, and ichthyosaurs), to the hugely abundant ammonites, as well as a great range of chalky planktonic organisms; while in the air the flying reptiles (pterosaurs) and enantiornithine birds disappeared forever.

Clearly it was necessary to try to understand what might have caused such a dramatic loss of life. The flip side of this general question was just as important: why did some creatures survive? After all, modern birds survived, so did mammals, and so did lizards and snakes, crocodiles and tortoises, fish and a whole host of other sea creatures. Was it just luck? Up until 1980, most of the theories that had been put forward to explain the K-T extinctions and survivals ranged from the sublime to the ridiculous.

One of the more persistent of the pre-1980 theories revolved around detailed studies of the ecological make-up of the time zones closest to the K-T boundary. The consensus suggested that there was a shift to progressively more seasonal/variable climatic conditions at the end of the Cretaceous Period. This was mirrored in the decline of those animals and plants less able to cope with more stressful climatic conditions. This was linked, rather inconclusively, to tectonic changes towards the close of the Cretaceous Period; these included marked sea-level rises and greatly increased continental provinciality. The general impression was that the world was slowly changing in character, and this eventually culminated in a dramatic faunal and floral turnover. Clearly such explanations require a longer timescale for the extinction event to take place, but the Achilles heel was that this did not adequately account for the simultaneous changes seen in marine communities. In the absence of better-quality data, arguments waxed and waned with no obvious resolution.

In 1980, this field of investigation was completely revolutionized by, of all people, an astronomer, Luis Alvarez. His son Walter, a palaeobiologist, had been studying changes in plankton diversity at the K-T boundary. It seemed logical to assume that the interval between the Late Cretaceous and Early Tertiary might simply represent a longish period of 'missing' time – a genuine gap in the continuity of the fossil record. To assist Walter in his studies concerning the changes in planktonic communities at this critical time in Earth history, Luis suggested that he could measure the amount of cosmic dust that was accumulating in boundary sediments in order to be able to provide an estimate of the extent of this presumed geological gap. Their results shocked the palaeontological and geological world. They found that the boundary layer, which was represented by a thin band of clay, contained enormous quantities of cosmic debris that could only be explained by the impact and subsequent vaporization of a gigantic meteorite. They calculated that this meteorite would have needed to be at least 10 kilometres in diameter. Considering the effect of the impact of such a giant meteorite, they further proposed that the huge debris cloud generated (containing water vapour and dust particles) after the impact would have shrouded the Earth completely for a significant period of time, perhaps several months or even a year or two. Shrouding the Earth in this way would have shut down photosynthesis of land plants and planktonic organisms, and triggered the simultaneous collapse of terrestrial and aquatic ecosystems. At a stroke, the Alvarezes and their colleagues seemed to have found a unifying explanation for the K-T event.

As with all good theories, the impact hypothesis generated an impressive volume of research. Throughout the 1980s, more and more teams of researchers were able to identify cosmic debris and violent impact-related signals in K-T boundary sediments from the four corners of the globe. By the late 1980s, the attention of a number of workers was drawn to the Caribbean area. Reports showed that on some of the Caribbean islands, such as Haiti, deposits of sediments at the K-T boundary not only showed the impact signal, but immediately above this an enormous thickness of breccia (broken masses of rock that had been thrown together). This, as well as the greater thicknesses of the meteorite debris layer and its chemical signature, prompted the suggestion that the meteorite had impacted somewhere in the shallow sea in this area. In 1991, the announcement was made that researchers had identified a large subterranean meteorite impact crater, which they called Chicxulub, on the Yucatán Peninsula of Mexico. The crater itself had been covered by 65 million years of sediment, and had only been visualized by studying seismic echoes of the Earth's crust (rather like the principle of underground radar). The crater appeared to be approximately 200 kilometres across and coincided with the K-T boundary layer, so Alvarez's theory was vindicated in a most remarkable way.

From the early 1990s onwards, study of the K-T event shifted away from the causes, which then seemed to have been established, to attempting to link the extinctions at this time to a single catastrophic event. The parallels to the nuclear winter debate are fairly clear. Advances in computer modelling, combined with knowledge of the likely chemical composition of the 'target' rocks (shallow sea deposits) and their behaviour under high-pressure shock, have shed light on the early phases of the impact and its environmental effects. At Yucatán, the meteorite would have impacted on a sea floor that was naturally rich in water, carbonate, and sulphate; this would have propelled as much as 200 gigatons *each* of sulphur dioxide and water vapour into the stratosphere. Impact models based on the geometry of the crater itself suggest that the impact was oblique and from the south-east. This trajectory would have concentrated the expelled gases towards North America. The fossil record certainly suggests that floral extinctions were particularly severe in this area, but more work elsewhere is needed before this pattern can be verified. Alvarez and others' work on the effects of the impact suggested that dust and clouds would have plunged the world into a freezing blackout. However, computer modelling of atmospheric conditions now suggests that within a few months light levels and temperatures would have begun to rebound because of the thermal inertia of the oceans, and the steady fall-out of particulate matter from the atmosphere. Unfortunately, however, things would have become no better for some considerable time because the sulphur dioxide and water in the atmosphere would have combined to produce sulphuric acid aerosols, and these would have severely reduced the amount of sunlight reaching the Earth's surface for between 5 and 10 years. These aerosols would have had the combined effects of cooling the Earth to near freezing and drenching the surface in acid rain.

Clearly these estimates are based only on computer models, which may be subject to error. However, even if only partly true, the general scope of the combination of environmental effects following the impact would have been genuinely devastating, and may well account for many aspects of the terrestrial and marine extinctions that mark the end of the Cretaceous Period. In a sense, the wonder is that anything survived these apocalyptic conditions at all.

Perturbations

While much of the work in recent years has focused on explaining the environmental effects of a large meteorite on global ecosystems, work is still continuing at the Chicxulub site. A major borehole has now been sunk into the crater to a depth of 1.5 kilometres in order that detailed examination of the impact zone can take place. What is beginning to emerge is slightly disturbing to the general pattern that has been explained above. One set of interpretations of the core data indicates that the impact crater may have been made as many as 300,000 years *before* the K-T boundary. The interval is represented by 0.5 metres of sediment. This evidence has been used to propose that the end Cretaceous event was not focused on a single large meteorite impact, but several large impacts that occurred right up to the K-T boundary – the cumulative effect of which may have caused the pattern of extinctions.

Clearly these new findings indicate that more research and more debate will undoubtedly take place in years to come. Not least among these are the data concerning massive volcanic activity that coincided with the end Cretaceous events. Parts of India known as the Deccan represent a gigantic series of flood-basalts that have been estimated as representing millions of cubic kilometres. Quite what the environmental impact of such enormous volcanic outpourings was, and whether this was in any way linked to the meteorite impact on the other side of the world, is still to be established.

Mass extinctions are fascinating punctuation marks in the history of life on Earth – nailing down exactly what caused them is, not surprisingly, very difficult.

Dinosaur research now and in the near future

It should be clear by now that a subject such as palaeobiology – certainly as it is currently being applied to fascinating creatures such as dinosaurs – has a decided unpredictability about it. Many research programmes in palaeobiology can be planned, and indeed have an intellectually satisfying structure to them, in order to explore specific issues or problems; this is normal for all the sciences. However, serendipity also plays a significant role: it can lead research in unexpected directions that could not have been anticipated at the outset. It can also be influenced strongly by spectacular new discoveries – nobody in the early 1990s would have been able to predict the amazing 'dinobird' finds that were made in China in 1996 and continue to the present day; technological advances in the physical and biological sciences also play an increasingly important part in research, allowing us to study fossils in ways that were, again, unimaginable just a few years ago.

To take advantage of many of these opportunities it is important to have at hand people who share a number of characteristics. Above all, they need to have an abiding interest in the history of life on Earth and naturally inquisitive temperaments. They also need some training in a surprisingly wide range of areas. While there is still an importance in the individual scientist working and thinking creatively in some degree of isolation, it is increasingly the case that multidisciplinary teams are needed to bring a wider range of skills to bear on each problem, or each new discovery, in order to tease out the information that will move the science a little further forward.

And finally . . .

My message is a relatively simple one. We, as a human race, could simply chose to ignore the history of life on Earth, as can be interpreted, in part at least, through the study of fossils. There are indeed many who adhere to such thoughts. Fortunately, I would say, a few of us do not. The pageant of life has been played out across the past 3,600 million years – a staggeringly long period of time. We as humans currently dominate most ecosystems, either directly or indirectly, but we have only risen to this position over the past 10,000 years of life on Earth. Before the human species, a wide range of organisms held sway. The dinosaurs were one such group and they, in a sense, acted as unwitting custodians of the Earth they inhabited. Palaeobiology allows us to trace parts of that custodianship.

The deeper question is: can we learn from past experiences and use them to help us to preserve an inhabitable Earth for other species to inherit when we are finally gone? This is an awesome responsibility given the current global threats posed by an exponential population increase, climatic change, and the threat posed by nuclear power. We are the first species ever to exist on this planet that has been able to appreciate that the Earth is not just 'here and now' but has a deep history. I hope sincerely that we will not also be the last. The one thing that we can be sure of, after studying the waxing and waning of species throughout the immensity of the fossil record, is that the human species will not endure for ever.

From our origins as *Homo sapiens* approximately 500,000 years ago, our species might last a further 1 million years, or perhaps even 5 million years if we are extraordinarily successful (or lucky), but we will eventually go the way of the dinosaurs: that much at least is written in the rocks.

Further reading

D. E. G. Briggs and P. R. Crowther (eds), *Palaeobiology II* (Oxford: Blackwell Science, 2001)

C. R. Darwin, *On the Origin of Species by Means of Natural Selection, or the Preservation of Favoured Races in the Struggle for Life* (London: John Murray, 1859)

R. De Salle and D. Lindley, *The Science of Jurassic Park and the Lost World, or How to Build a Dinosaur* (London: Harper Collins, 1997)

D. R. Dean, *Gideon Mantell and the Discovery of Dinosaurs* (Cambridge: Cambridge University Press, 1999)

A. J. Desmond, *The Hot-Blooded Dinosaurs: A Revolution in Palaeontology* (London: Blond & Briggs, 1975)

C. Lavers, *Why Elephants Have Big Ears* (London: Gollancz, 2000)

A. Mayor, *The First Fossil Hunters: Palaeontology in Greek and Roman Times* (Princeton: Princeton University Press, 2001)

C. McGowan, *The Dragon Seekers* (Cambridge, MA: Perseus Publishing, 2001)

D. B. Norman, *Dinosaur!* (London: Boxtree, 1991)

D. B. Norman, *Prehistoric Life: The Rise of the Vertebrates* (London: Boxtree, 1994)

D. B. Norman and P. Wellnhofer, *The Illustrated Encyclopedia of Dinosaurs* (London: Salamander Books, 2000)

M. J. S. Rudwick, *The Meaning of Fossils: Episodes in the History of Palaeontology* (New York: Science History Books, 1976)

D. B. Weishampel, P. Dodson, *et al.* (eds), *The Dinosauria* (Berkeley and Los Angeles: University of California Press, 2004)

Index

Index

Expand your collection of
VERY SHORT INTRODUCTIONS

Visit the
VERY SHORT
INTRODUCTIONS
Web site

www.oup.co.uk/vsi

➤ **Information** about all published titles

➤ News of **forthcoming books**

➤ **Extracts** from the books, including titles
  not yet published

➤ **Reviews** and views

➤ **Links** to other **web sites** and main
  OUP web page

➤ Information about **VSIs in translation**

➤ **Contact** the editors

➤ **Order** other **VSIs** on-line

ARCHAEOLOGY
A Very Short Introduction
Paul Bahn

This entertaining Very Short Introduction reflects the enduring popularity of archaeology – a subject which appeals as a pastime, career, and academic discipline, encompasses the whole globe, and surveys 2.5 million years. From deserts to jungles, from deep caves to mountain tops, from pebble tools to satellite photographs, from excavation to abstract theory, archaeology interacts with nearly every other discipline in its attempts to reconstruct the past.

'very lively indeed and remarkably perceptive ... a quite brilliant and level-headed look at the curious world of archaeology'

Barry Cunliffe, University of Oxford

'It is often said that well-written books are rare in archaeology, but this is a model of good writing for a general audience. The book is full of jokes, but its serious message – that archaeology can be a rich and fascinating subject – it gets across with more panache than any other book I know.'

Simon Denison, editor of *British Archaeology*

www.oup.co.uk/vsi/archaeology